WHY VEGAN

WHY VEGAN

A NEW FOOD BOOK
BY
KATH CLEMENTS

First published November 1985 by GMP Publishers Ltd,
  P O Box 247, London N15 6RW.
World copyright © Kath Clements 1985.
Illustrations world copyright © Jeff King 1985.

British Library Cataloguing in Publication Data

  Clements, Kath
    Why Vegan — (A Heretic book)
    1. Vegetarianism
    I. Title
    613.2'62   RM236

  ISBN 0-946097-18-6

Illustrated by Jeff King
Typeset by Ramsey Margolis/Artworkers, London
Printed and bound by Billing & Sons Ltd, Worcester

1. Why Vegan?

Food is a subject close to everyone's hearts, whether they admit it or not. It should be a happy subject, connoting fulfilment of one of our basic appetites and happy times with families and friends. But the first part of this book is about our responsibility through the food we eat for exploitation and suffering in the world today, which is not a happy subject. It is an attempt to persuade and enable more people to adopt a diet which excludes animal products. It is aimed at 'the general reader', as there are much better specialist books dealing with each topic it covers (see Bibliography), and it is short, to save time and paper.

(i) Vegan – The Word

The word 'vegan' was coined in 1945 by the newly-formed Vegan Society to describe those who avoid animal products for food, clothing and other consumer goods. There were numbers of people who took the step for their own ethical reasons (we shall never know how many) with no knowledge of the Vegan Society or this new word, and some who were glad to find out about it later, with its support and guidance. Over the years many have been helped and enlightened by the Vegan Society, including myself.

Thousands now follow a vegan diet without the need for special guidance, the feeling of taking a fairly drastic step, or being considered a race apart from the normal run of humanity. But because of a smear on the word 'vegan', which has come about in various subtle ways, the word sometimes can be made to sound rather like an aberration, and in the normal course I would rarely use it. However, for convenience I will use it here.

Vegans, of course, are individuals with their own ideals and varying reasons for adopting their diet and lifestyle. This little book is an attempt to explain the main reasons, from one vegan's viewpoint, and to suggest some ideas about food and meals.

Veganism is not about cats' homes and being kind to furry animals, about living in cloud cuckoo-land where nature's cycle of destruction and creation can somehow be avoided. Vegans do not imagine that their food bypasses every possibility of death and suffering for the animal kingdom. The grain fields needed for the bread we eat rob many animals of their natural habitats and mean that many more are killed as pests. It is not necessarily compassion for animals alone which leads people to veganism. But veganism is about having a consistent approach to human rights and animal rights, ecology and world food problems. It is a very important subject indeed, since each of us is responsible through what we consume for the management of the Earth's resources, and ultimately for peaceful coexistence with others on the planet.

(ii) World Food

A prime reason for veganism is the desperate nature of the world food situation. The threat of destruction of the world through atomic fission hovers over us and we fear for our children's future, yet millions are already watching their children starve to death in conditions similar to a post-holocaust famine. Despite the fact that the world production of wheat alone is 1 kg. per day for every person alive (according to a recent Oxfam hand-out), twelve to thirteen million children die each year through malnutrition; that is the equivalent of a Hiroshima every three days. Since at least the early sixties, through media coverage, we have been aware of the extreme poverty of the Third World, though profiteers and politicians in our own country encourage us unceasingly to hope for even higher standards of living for ourselves.

POPULATION OF BRITAIN	
Human	56 million
Cattle	14 million
Sheep	28 million
Pigs	8 million
Poultry	142 million

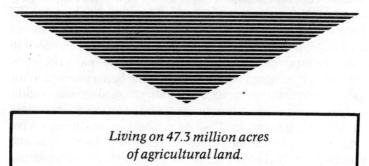

Living on 47.3 million acres
of agricultural land.

It is the over-consumption of meat, eggs and dairy products in the West that underlies the inequitable distribution of the world's food resources, because as well as feeding ourselves, we in the affluent countries are feeding a huge population of farm animals. *(Fig. 1.)* But colossal vested interests on the one hand, and blinkered table habits on the other, encourage us to continue in ignorance of the facts. The facts are that our farm animals are often fed on vegetable protein suitable for direct human consumption, and often their feedstuff is of Third World origin. If the world is divided into rich North and poor South, the model taken by the Brandt Report of 1978, then for every well-fed person in this country there are ten hungry ones in the poor world. Each Northerner consumes five times as much grain as a Southerner, and most of this grain is fed to animals.[1]

(iii) The Meat and Milk Myth

Animal products are not even necessary in any proportion in our diet, though the large majority of British people are convinced that meat, milk, and eggs are natural, healthy and needed to sustain human life. But farming has become extremely unnatural and its products far less healthy in order to feed our large urban populations on animal protein. The belief in the almost magical properties of meat and milk is deeply rooted in our culture. There are social and historical reasons for it, dating back to times when only the rich could afford to eat much meat. People ate meat less often and their small portion was indeed the richest thing on their plate. Farms were smaller and used organic methods which are no longer economically viable, so the meat was a chemically different product. And history shows that people have eaten increasingly large amounts of meat. From being a rare treat for the common people in mediaeval times, consumption of meat has increased over the centuries with the rising expectations of working people, until we now have a situation where someone might eat meat three times a day. And in Eastern Europe, after the liberation from serfdom, meat-eating became much more widespread because it symbolised the rich life of the old ruling classes; now all the working people consider meat a vital part of their 'rights' and will queue for hours to demonstrate it, whilst the Soviet Union is in the precarious situation of having to import vast amounts of grain to feed its farm animals for slaughter.

The demand for meat is behind the whole economic set-up. But the belief in meat and milk is nothing but a myth, a massive con-trick perpetuated by massive vested interests. I call it the meat and milk myth.

In this country, the government has been bolstering the farming industry since the last war, and in recent times Europe's Common Agricultural Policy, by assuring farmers of being able to sell their produce at a good price regardless of demand, has created estimated surpluses of 600,000 tonnes of butter, 6,297,000 tonnes of wheat and 1,500,000 tonnes of barley (1983). The latest figures I have seen estimate that the EEC beef mountain is *growing* at the rate of 25,000 tonnes per *week* and creating acute storage problems.[2] The effect of the Common Agricultural Policy is in fact to protect European farmers at the expense of Third World producers.

The National Farmers Union is an enormously powerful body, and it is no accident that many cabinet members of whatever party are found to be farmers (one-third of the cabinet at the time of writing, and fifty MPs). Over recent years, as farmers' incomes have been increasing along with European food mountains and lakes, allocations of aid to the poor countries have declined. About two-thirds of the EEC budget goes on agriculture, and until recently there have been no constraints on over-production, as with other industries of national importance. In the UK even poorer farmers benefit from rate and tax exemptions, including VAT. Government subsidies which began in wartime to keep food prices down now exist largely to protect the farmers' interests. The government now seems to be realising that it cannot continue pouring such vast amounts of our money into the farming industry, but it is unlikely that the powerful landowning interests which have developed meanwhile will voluntarily release their hold on the strings which boost their income.

At the moment, the economics of our country is geared to meat production whether we like it or not, and we are all paying for it through taxation. But the system relies heavily on imports (we produce a large proportion of our meat but the animal feed has to be imported), it worsens food shortages in other parts of the world, and it increases the likelihood of war. That's how serious it is.

Now for a closer look at the inefficiency, in real terms, of modern farming, and at some of the powerful interests that keep it going.

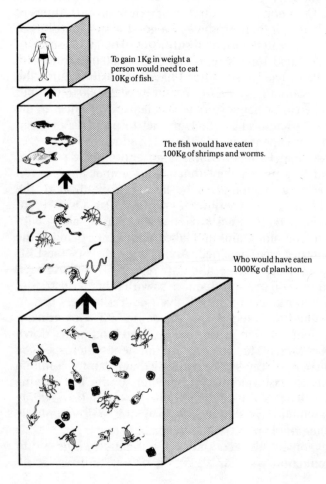

To gain 1Kg in weight a person would need to eat 10Kg of fish.

The fish would have eaten 100Kg of shrimps and worms.

Who would have eaten 1000Kg of plankton.

10

Figure 2

2. The Food Industry

'500 million people – the equivalent of the total population of Europe – are being deprived of one of the most basic needs: food. For any change to take place, we must first recognise that it is the present system of world food production and distribution which is failing disastrously.'

Nigel Twose, *Cultivating Hunger*

'People are beginning to wake up to the absurdity of wasting our resources and impoverishing our soil to produce food that cannot be used within the straitjacket of our economic system.'

K. Jannaway
(former Secretary, Vegan Society)

(i) The True Cost of Meat

That meat is a wasteful way of producing food protein is beyond doubt. Weight for weight, there is only about a 10 per cent conversion rate from plant to animal protein (less if you count how much of the product is unusable or wasted) which means that it takes an awful lot of plant material to produce a certain amount of steak, eggs or milk.

Figures vary, of course, but it is noticeable how often this ratio of approximately ten to one keeps recurring in studies of

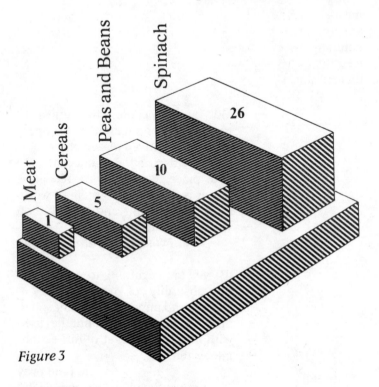

Ratio of protein values produced from a given piece of land

Meat

Cereals

Peas and Beans

Spinach

1

5

10

26

Figure 3

food returns. For instance, using body weight as a measure, one study has shown that it would take ten kilos of fish to make a person gain one kilo in weight. The fish would have consumed 100 kilos of shrimp and worms, and the shrimp and worms 1,000 kilos of plankton. So one kilo of the person's body weight represents one tonne of matter two steps further down the food chain! *(Fig. 2.)* (This example is used by Kit Pedler in his book *The Quest for Gaia* – see Bibliography.) Again, using land as a measure of efficiency, cereals produce five times as much protein as meat, peas and beans ten times more and spinach twenty-six times more.[3] *(Fig. 3.)*

Another estimate has shown that soya beans can produce 260 kg. of protein per acre, lucerne 675 kg. per acre and prime grade beef only 49 kg. per acre.[4] *(Fig. 4)*

So it takes approximately five times as much land to feed a meat-eater as it does a vegetarian. Now, if you have a limited amount of land, and a growing number of people, you would naturally use that land in the most efficient way in order to feed the people – unless you deliberately intended some of them to starve.

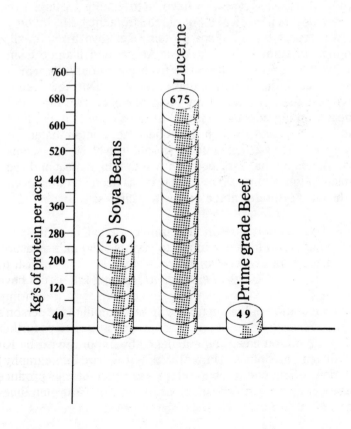

Figure 4

In terms of our farming industry's efficiency, there is also to be considered the cost in energy of shipping animal feed halfway around the world and of running the intensive units which comprise the majority of modern-day farms. For years we have been conscious of this wastefulness, as newspaper articles over the last decade or so have shown. The economic facts now indicate that we simply shall not be able to afford it for much longer.

If the balance of payments is a concern of British politicians, they could do worse than reduce the amount we spend on imported animal feedstuffs. In 1983 the EEC imported 14 million tonnes of grain just to feed animals. Britain alone imports 4 million of the 14 million tonnes of grain to feed its livestock each year.[5] Yet 92 per cent of farmland in the UK is already devoted to feeding livestock (we import most of the wheat for our bread from the US). Not only do we import lots of plant protein, e.g. soya from Brazil, ground-nut from India and West Africa, and manioc from Thailand, but most of it comes from poor countries which have a vast indigenous population to feed. During a recent fowl pest scare, I read in my local paper of 'rice bran and wheat bran ingredients imported from Pakistan, the Far East and other places' which had become contaminated at Liverpool. That chicken feed should travel so far seems absurd, when it has long been known that high meat and egg consumption is unnecessary and this has been admitted even in the most orthodox and conservative circles:

> 'Food imports are, in fact, unnecessary. Our farm land is productive enough to support 250 million people on a vegetarian diet.'
> *British Medical Journal,* July 1977

(The population of Britain now is under 60 millions.)

We are not only causing imbalance by importing precious food from parts of the Third World, but we are encouraging the developing countries to adopt our wasteful regime. For instance, Egypt was self-sufficient in food in 1970, but now imports 70 per cent. The Egyptian government realises the

14

potential danger of this situation and is trying to remedy it, unfortunately with highly sophisticated imported methods which may ultimately fail. The Soviet Union, too, is a large food importer and buys up a quarter of the world's exported wheat and butter (most of the latter from the USA, by the way, but via New Zealand ...). This is a situation which could prove explosive at times of international tension.

(ii) Multinationals and Monopolies

> 'The food producers monopoly exceeds the oil producers monopoly.'
> US Assistant Secretary of State, 1974

Just as the problem is one of world dimensions, the forces behind it are vast. 370 million tonnes of animal feed per year are fed to farm animals in the West, an amount equivalent to the total consumption of the people of India and China.[6] The grain shipments that we occasionally make to a Third World country when famine is in the news and our conscience is pricked are a worthless fraction of the amounts we store and import to feed our immense population of farm animals. Huge multinationals, like Nestlés, Unilever, Spillers French and Rank Hovis McDougal, are in control of the rearing, transport and slaughter of the billions of head of livestock in the USA and Europe. Often the farmers are contract growers and what they grow bears little relation to local demand.

But the farmers themselves are not in control of the industry. Huge powers indeed lie behind the meat and milk myth, and the network of vested interests behind them is complex. For instance, there is a known correlation between consumption of animal fats and the incidence of heart disease. Ten years ago, when the DHSS Committee on Medical Aspects of Food Policy (COMA) published its first report on diet and coronary heart disease, it was so reserved in its condemnation of saturated fats as a cause of heart disease that a Dutch professor of nutrition wrote that Britain would act as a control against which other countries could measure their success in reducing heart disease. Unfortunately this has

15

proved correct since, whilst several other countries have significantly reduced heart disease by public education, in Britain more than one in every three people die from cerebrovascular disease or coronary heart disease. This is the world's highest rate. COMA therefore produced a second report in August 1984, which seems however to be more concerned with its own scientific reputation than with bringing about a successful public education programme. The leaders of the food industry have welcomed the caginess of the COMA report which suggests only that the fat content of foods should be shown 'wherever practicable', and now the producers are already introducing their own code of labelling which draws attention away from fat content. Once again the profit motive overrides health considerations.

(iii) The Great Con-Trick

The British Nutrition Foundation, one of the supposed guardians of our health, is itself largely a creation of the food manufacturing industry. In a 1982 report, *Implementation of Dietary Guidelines: Obstacles and Opportunities*, the following passage is found:

> 'Any consideration of national dietary guidelines must take account of this economic colossus [the food industry] ... The prime industries provide employment for over two million people, have huge sums invested in them and are a major factor in the economic health of the nation ... Simply to say "let there be substantially less sugar or butter", for example, would have far-reaching economic implications worldwide.'

The vested interests are admitted and the organisation is condemned by its own words.

It is now becoming clear that actual manipulation of official programmes has taken place. *The Food Scandal*, a recent book by Caroline Walker and Geoffrey Cannon (see Bibliography), describes how the National Advisory Council on

Nutrition Education, which the government set up in 1979, was obstructed by the agriculturalists and food manufacturers so that its final report became too obscure to be of much use to the general public. With such forces at work, the economic set-up goes ambling on, the government subsidies continue to produce surpluses of unhealthy produce, and the meat and milk myth is perpetuated.

(iv) Politics and Food Mountains

America, too, has its food mountains (which make ours look like molehills), created by the forces of world politics and economics, including Europe's CAP. Below the ground in Kansas City is the country's largest 'Commercial Distribution Center', where the trucks line up to dump endless tons of cereal grains which can't immediately be sold. After the invasion of Afghanistan, the Carter administration stopped exporting grain to the Soviet Union, which later responded by not buying US products. The whole thing was a disaster for American farmers, who now resent having to compete in the world market with European products, which, unlike theirs, have a heavy government subsidy. So America's huge cereal output goes to waste, and meanwhile our own farmers are ploughing up yet more of our irreplaceable countryside because of the artificially high price of wheat in the EEC. Of course, these lunacies are not necessarily caused entirely by our meat-based diet; but operations which rely on the shipment of such huge amounts of feed for livestock, where large investments are involved, are bound to get out of hand. And we can be certain that handsome profits have been made whilst the food mountains have been accumulating.

3. Down on the Farm

(i) Factory Farming

Despite the absurdities of Western food production, there are still many who think that modern developments are our main hope for feeding our huge populations. Factory farming, for instance, was hailed as a necessary evil which was to alleviate food shortages by confining farming operations into a smaller space. But confined animals take an even higher proportion of their food from good arable land than do animals which roam in the fields. In close confinement, the health and vitality of the animals suffer, and so does the product. Reliance on drugs and additives to combat infection and enhance profitability increases artificial residues in the products and heightens the risk to the consumer, since farm animals can and do exchange drug-resistant bacteria. (This is the product, saturated with drugs and hormones, that the myth encourages us to consider the mainstay of our lives!) Also, factory farms maintain their controlled environments by heavy dependence on hardware and energy resources; and heavy concentrations of animal waste cause environmental problems of air and water pollution.

(ii) Dairy Farming

But surely, you may say, we can still have milk and other dairy produce, since cows produce it so abundantly it must make good sense for us to drink it. Unfortunately (for the cows) this is not the case, since lactation occurs only in the period following the birth of a calf. A cow gives as milk only about one-tenth of the protein she eats, and the modern dairy industry involves an extremely artificial and intensive use of resources. Partly by genetic manipulation, and partly by feeding hormone stimulants and food concentrates, the annual production of a typical cow has been increased from 1,500 litres of milk in 1950 to over 5,000 litres in 1983.[7] Mere grazing in the meadows does not produce such yields. The methods of modern dairy farming are a very expensive way of producing a European surplus of one million tonnes of skimmed milk and a butter mountain which costs us £500,000 per day to store.[8] Recent restrictions in subsidy will only reduce and not eliminate this surplus.

In any case, the dairy industry is really part and parcel of the beef industry, with 80 per cent of beef now sold being a by-product of dairy farms. The calf which each cow has to produce each year to maintain her milk supply will either be slaughtered very early for veal, or go to a veal unit or a beef herd; a minority of females become part of another dairy herd. The fuss that the farmers made when the milk 'quotas' were imposed in 1984 played heavily on the public ignorance of these facts; the farmers wept crocodile tears at having to send cows to slaughter to cut their losses – as if the cows were not going to die anyway, at the moment most convenient to the farmer, and as if milk production itself did not rely on the mass slaughter of calves. The myth is so strong that the public continues to be conned by the crocodile tears; in Cornwall, where I live, there are car stickers to be seen with the message 'Save Cows – Drink Milk'!

Incidentally, there are more bizarre ways to off-load surpluses in the dairy industry than the flavoured drinks now being produced. Currently in Devon, as a local paper reports, waste whey from cheese-making is simply dumped over the fields; and at Haslington, near Crewe, a factory has been switched to converting whey for use by the pharmaceutical trade in pill-making.[9] In recent years, whey has popped up in various surprising places in foods which are not normally associated with milk, as habitual readers of food labels will realise. In terms of the Earth's resources, the dairy industry is responsible for a colossal amount of wastage.

(iii) Animal Waste

One aspect of the wastage is the slurry produced by the dairy farms. Advocates of animal farming would say that animal rearing is necessary so that the animals' dung can keep the soil in good heart. Indeed, in the natural course of events both animal and human waste would be returned as nutrients to the soil by the process of decay. But so much animal waste is produced by intensive farming that it is impossible to return it to the land locally and it is either transported elsewhere, dumped in waterways or simply burned so that it is totally wasted.

Far from being good for the land, modern husbandry is a major pollutant of the country's water systems. In 1982, 2,523 cases of pollution from farms were reported to water authorities in this country,[10] and many more no doubt went unreported. This is in addition to the chemical spin-off from farms, which is responsible for the alarming amounts of nitrates in our drinking water.

Human waste is obviously available if necessary to maintain the health of the soil, and surely the possibility of infections and poisoning (as with factory farming) is something that our advanced technology can deal with. In any event, animal waste is not necessarily a vital ingredient of crop-growing. In demonstration of this, a farmer called Manfred Wenz, on his 32 hectares near Strasbourg, has been successfully practising organic stockless farming for twelve years, and with crop rotation and green manuring grows rye, wheat and beans with yields comparable with those of his neighbours, without the use of animal manure. (There are details of this in publications of the Vegan Society and the Henry Doubleday Research Association.)

(iv) Healthy Soil and Healthy Landscape

In this country there are many gardens which use 'veganic' methods (with no animal waste), and some of the more methodical of these have been monitored by an offshoot of the Vegan Society. There must be thousands more back gardens which benefit from a compost heap but otherwise no imported animal waste (including bone meal etc.) and keep the soil in excellent health with the aid of the micro-organisms and wild creatures that naturally inhabit it. Only compare the delight of spreading sweet-smelling compost over your garden with the unpleasant experience of being near a field where muck-spreading is taking place, to see the case for veganic methods. Traditionally, animal manure has been the way of maintaining soil fertility on Britain's smaller mixed farms, but those days are a long way behind us. Nowadays, the typical modern farm has reached 4,000 acres in extent.[11] Soil fertility is maintained courtesy of ICI and others, and animal slurry is an embarrassment to the farmer.

I am convinced that soil fertility can be maintained by compost growing, crop rotation, green manuring, and the careful recycling of human waste. Given this situation, our 'overcrowded' island would have no difficulty feeding itself on a vegan diet, as was shown by a study undertaken under the auspices of Professor Watkin Williams, head of the

22

Department of Agriculture and Botany at Reading University (see also Kenneth Mellanby's *Can Britain Feed Itself?* – Bibliography).

The vegan landscape would include many trees as a prime renewable source of food as well as fuel. For instance, 'the yield per acre of well-managed hazel trees may reach at least two tons, though average yields still range from 6-10 cwts per acre'.[12] In fact, a far larger amount of food per acre can be produced by tree-growing than by any other means. Walnuts, for instance, have an astonishingly high food value to man, supplying many essential nutrients. 'An acre of walnuts will supply more than 1,000 lbs of shelled meats with a food value of 3,000,000 calories. This is 20 times the amount that the same acre would yield in beef. The protein quality of the nuts would be as great as in beef and of superior quality.'[13] In addition, exciting possibilities could unfold if the food technology that has developed around the soya bean were adapted to British crops. And interesting projects such as paper-making from fast-growing crops could develop, again saving millions of pounds per year on timber imports.

(v) Necessary Changes

Instead of the present cutting-back of the work done in such places as the East Malling Research Station in Kent, world famous for growing root stocks for fruit, such work should be encouraged as a priority; it is time to cut back instead on the ghastly research programmes which have produced such pathologically huge cattle, such unnaturally lean pigs and such amazingly prolific hens. If we, the consumers, create new market demands, refusing to be brainwashed by the Meat Promotion Executive's desperate bid to recapture its dwindling market, the ingenious farmers will just have to respond by producing every type of cereal, vegetable, fruit and pulse that our climate allows. They could find new sources of income and opportunities for cash crop growing and syndicate operation even within the present economic set-up.

I believe, however, that in the interests of the world's poor (i.e. the majority) the economic system itself will one day have to change. We may be led to believe that foreign exchange is necessary for the economic development of the poor countries, but it seems in fact that foreign exchange provides the poor countries only with such fruits of civilisation as advanced weaponry, Coca-Cola and powdered infant 'food'. In fact the foreign exchange system is closely linked with the increasing poverty and militarisation of the Third World. As the poor countries get deeper and deeper into debt at the whim of currency exchange rates, more land is given over to cash crop growing instead of feeding the people,[14] so more arms are needed to suppress the dispossessed poor, so the national debt increases, etc. in a very vicious circle *(Fig. 5)*. Aid programmes which encourage self-sufficiency at grass-roots level (not state-backed technical projects which are in fact a corrupt form of investment) seem to be the only rays of hope at the moment.

Land reform and a return to indigenous farming methods and diet might help the poor countries much more than introducing the mechanical toys of our technocracy which are expensive to run and maintain. Ghostly ruins of massive trucks and tractors stand amidst the newly desert land of Burkina Faso (Upper Volta) as a monument to an attempt to import Texan ranching methods into the region; whilst since independence that country's coffee and cotton exports have increased by 32 per cent (not necessarily generating a commensurate increase of income) and food production for local consumption has not increased at all.[15]

The Poverty-Repression-Militarisation Cycle

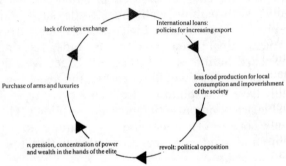

Figure 5 (reproduced from *Bombs for Breakfast*, see Bibliography)

24

4. Ecological Aspects

'If animals and vegetables do have a basic right to life, simply by virtue of existence and occupancy of the planet, then it follows that the number of deaths we cause by eating should be kept to a minimum. Again this is not a moral statement, it is related to survival and the need to reconnect our way of life to the cycles of solar absorption, growth and decay. To interfere as little as possible seems to be commensurate with long-term survival.'

Kit Pedler

(i) The Land

Our civilisation has disrupted the traditional cultures of three continents and replaced them with exploitation and new, unviable systems in order to produce raw materials for our advanced stage of consumerism. At the same time, our rich Western diet, which concentrates on animal farming, has drastically changed the appearance of our own landscape. Primaeval forest once covered nearly all the land surface of Britain, up to 600 metres above sea level.

There are those who defend animal farming on the grounds that animals can feed on grasslands and in hill country unsuitable for arable crops, and on plants unsuitable for human digestion, so that they have a valid place in the ecology of farming. However, in parts of the Third World, large-scale grazing of animals has contributed to the disastrous situations which prevail at present. The Sahara Desert itself is largely a creation of over-grazing. In Brazil, huge cattle ranches take up some of the most fertile soil in the whole country and even more forest land is being destroyed in order to produce meat for American beefburgers (though tropical grazing land thus created has a life of ten years at very best), whilst 60 per cent of Brazilians are malnourished. In Central American countries the situation is similar, with exports of beef cattle having increased five-fold.

In Britain as elsewhere, instead of grazing animals, we could plant trees where forests once grew and, unlike grazing animals, these would maintain the water table, preventing both drought and swamping, renew the purity of the air and the whole fertility of the land and viability of our large populations upon it. Animal manure is not necessary for soil fertility as long as crop rotation is practised and wastes are returned. On a small scale, putting a goat or two on a piece of rough land is an easy way out for people with no real love and understanding of the land; at the other end of the scale, hill farming as it is now practised is an absurdity that has cost us millions in government subsidies.

All our energy needs as well as food needs could be met, even with our relatively high population, if animal farming could be brought to an end. After all, grazing animals are the enemies of stable plant cover of the soil. Plants and especially trees are our most precious renewable resource, providing fuel, food, textiles, cosmetics and almost anything else that human ingenuity might devise. By biomass fermentation, 'all required liquid fuel could be obtained from 17 per cent of the UK's land area' and 'all gas from 15 per cent' (Professor David Hall of King's College, London, giving evidence at the Windscale Enquiry of 1977). The manufacture of fuel alcohol on a large scale has already been shown to be possible, for instance in Brazil, where part of the coffee crop is diverted in this way in order to lessen dependence on imported fuel (though unfortunately in this case it only runs cars for the rich). According to Professor Hall, this time addressing the Vegan Society in May 1984, all of the world's economically

extractable coal, oil and gas only have an energy content equal to that of the trees now growing in the world. This is in addition to the amazingly high potential as sources of essential nutrition of the nut and fruit bearing trees, referred to previously. It seems obvious that we should turn to trees as a more sound basis for our land husbandry and manufacturing.

A landscape not geared to the production of cash crops and animal feeds would consist of smaller fields of fruit, vegetables and cereals in rotation, surrounded by fruit and nut trees for protection, and trees for building materials and fuel, not to mention the possibilities for wild life and recreation that every country needs. This land could once again be green and pleasant, feeding our large population in the most economic, that is vegan, way. On a vegan diet, this small country could feed many more than its present population.

(ii) The Sea

Unfortunately, our dependence on animal products has not only disfigured and impoverished the land, but has drastically denatured the sea as well. Many 'vegetarians', for instance , will eat fish, saying perhaps to their conscience that fish are at least free-range. But the shoals of herring of our folk songs have been almost fished out of existence along with other once plentiful species. The fishermen are in serious trouble as fishing, like everything else, has become big business. But their plight is not half so serious as that of marine life itself. Japanese fishing fleets now use huge nets which stretch across hundreds of miles of ocean at a time, trapping as well as the fish millions (literally) of sea birds and marine animals in the fine mesh. Such seemingly far-off operations do not receive much public attention until a voluntary organisation like Greenpeace mounts a campaign, such as its monitoring in January 1984 of the salmon gill-netting operation in the Bering Sea. Fishing on such a horrific scale is what it is all about if we are to feed fish to our vast urban populations.

And yet the poorer nations are being encouraged to aspire to a Western-type diet with a heavy use of animal protein. To quote just two recent examples: delegates recently travelled from remote Third World countries to gather in Texas and learn about the intensive pig and cattle units there; battery farming of chickens is being developed in Bangladesh.[16] This of course is because certain rich nations are keen to boost their exports of technological gadgetry. As well as taking grain virtually from the mouths of the poor, such developments can only mean disaster for the world's resources. Attempts to make a diet based on animal foods available for everyone can only destroy the environment. On the other hand, it is not conducive to world harmony and peace to have such a diet available as at present only to the world's rich, for whom meat-eating has become a deeply entrenched habit. A lifetime of conditioning from all sides has encouraged such people to think of meat and milk as the best available food. But if the plight of the starving does not encourage them to rethink this, perhaps some healthy self-interest and knowledge of nutrition might do so.

5. Nutrition

'While people around us are dying like flies from heart disease, cancer, strokes, etc., and animals are being used in endless repetitive and useless experiments in an attempt to find "cures", the answer is under our very noses, right there on our plates in front of us at every meal.'

Jean Pink

(i) Our Natural Food

The fact is that our bodies seem to be 'designed' to be vegetarian, or, more accurately, like the great apes, to absorb a diet of fruit, nuts and shoots. We are not properly adapted to the consumption of flesh, far less the milk of other animals.

On a television chat show recently I watched a popular media figure, a botanist known for his love of steak, give out a diatribe of the variety: 'Haw haw, vegetarians have got it all wrong, anyone can see that horses' and cows' guts are far different from ours, we can't live on vegetables like the weak-kneed vegetarians, haw haw...' This is gross mis-information, and typical of the brain-washing that takes place. The meat myth is strong indeed when a 'scientist', watched by millions, can get away with such rubbish.

It is true that we are not like the herbivores, as anyone can see without even the need to slit one open to observe its copious entrails, developed for dealing with cellulose. Obviously we can't live on grass. But far from being akin to nature's carnivores, the pattern of organs in our bodies and the composition of our blood are identical with those of the great apes, i.e. the larger tail-less monkeys such as chimpanzees and gorillas.

Though modern-day researchers cannot be sure of human origins, it does seem likely that the traditional view of early man as a violent hunter has got it very wrong. The picture which has filled the early pages of many a school history book, of a club-bearing brute about to batter to death his next meal, is quite incorrect, though it might serve as a fitting model for the origins of a culture which has developed through belligerent self-interest. This is perfectly in line with the old school of history which has battles as its main landmarks, offering to young people stories of extreme brutality and selfishness (like the Wars of the Roses) as our 'heritage', rather than as something of which people, particularly the landed aristocracy, should be deeply ashamed.

As regards the origins of humankind, it is much more likely that we began as frugivorous creatures and took to flesh-eating only as a result of a migration to inhospitable regions, or a catastrophe like a drought or an ice age. In any event – and for whatever reason early humans 'broke the ancient primate habit of vegetarianism'[17] – in the light of what is now known about comparative physiology, and about early societies, the widely held assumptions about our origins as a primitive hunter and flesh-eater are probably incorrect. From teeth, jaws, and saliva right through the alimentary canal, our bodies are enormously different from those of the carnivores. We loosely call ourselves 'omnivorous', but that is through our own choice, not 'design'. Meat-eating nations have enormous health problems, with the so-called 'degenerative diseases', those caused by accumulations of wastes our bodies can't deal with, reaching epidemic proportions. After digestion in the intestines, meat becomes infested with putrefactive bacteria; carnivores have a short and smooth bowel for quick release of toxic wastes, unlike our own longer bowel. Healthy vegetarian mammals have much less noxious excretions than those of the omnivores!

(ii) Health Hazards of Meat and Milk

Nutritionists have known for decades about the possible harm of taking animal substances frequently into our bodies, but the knowledge filters very slowly through the entrenchments of our economic system and our table habits. The miraculous cleansing powers of our livers help to deal with the poisonous substances formed in the intestines of meat-eaters (skatole, indole, tryamine, phenylethylamine) and an active life in the fresh air helps too, but by the time we reach middle age most people are suffering to varying degrees from some chronic ailment. Obviously many more factors than diet affect our health, and the quality of the food in terms of soil fertility, chemical pollution and factory processing is very important as well as the type of diet itself; but I suspect that animal products per se, however wholesome or 'organic' the diet they comprise, have a deleterious effect on the human system.

The risk of bacterial infections alone is enough to make meat a highly suspect food. As soon as an animal's death occurs, putrefaction begins, and meat is by definition bound to be in some stage of (arrested) decay. Therefore meat as such is more akin to the carrion that nature's scavengers eat than to the fresh food of the hunting animals. Bacteria dangerous to humans such as salmonella are not found only in 'contaminated' meat but are among the many natural inhabitants of dead flesh. Only careful cooking and preserving can cheat the bacteria from entering our systems live, since we lack the adaptations of the carnivores to deal with them, such as the shorter bowel and the ten times greater internal secretions of hydrochloric acid. A substance which can so quickly become actually harmful to us, and which needs such careful treatment, can hardly be considered our 'natural' food. The last remnants of the disease-ridden Eskimo culture, with their high meat intake, are a very poor advertisement indeed for the diet.[18]

The high concentrations of protein and fat in a diet based on meat are mainly what is blamed for our modern 'diseases of affluence'. This is hardly surprising, since the stock raised on our farms is fattened for the meat wholesaler. Meat-eaters are not healthy animals, but 'pathologically fat-loaded beasts' (Dr Alex Comfort's words). Prime grade beef contains 63 per cent more fat than the standard grades [19] – fat which surrounds each muscle fibre and which is put there in the special 'finishing' process of overfeeding prior to slaughter in order to get most money for the beast. The animals have, moreover, almost certainly received large doses of synthetic hormones and antibiotics, which are passed on to the consumer. It is hardly surprising that our health service is so over-strained.

Our high consumption of milk (Britain consumes more milk than any other European nation) is another of the national habits which has arguably had a harmful effect on our health. If our bodies are demonstrably not perfectly adapted to meat consumption, they are far less adapted to drinking the milk of another species, an aberrant activity when you come to think about it. Milk is an infant food and humans are the only adult animal to take it. (Country tales of hedgehogs 'stealing' milk from cows' udders – i.e. stealing it from us, not the cow! – are largely exaggerated, if not completely fictitious.) The subject of nutrition is infinitely complicated and full of uncertainties, but the one certainty we do have is that human breast milk is specifically developed for feeding human infants, and is perfect for the job. Beyond that, the certainty ends, but investigations show that drinking cows' milk is not a healthy way of obtaining the protein, calcium and so on that it contains. The product of lactation of another animal has a composition very different from that of our more natural food (not to mention the artificial substances that the farmer has added) and our digestions cannot really cope with it.

After infancy, the enzymes necessary to digest milk disappear from our bodies. The various complications that then arise when milk is drunk, dubbed 'allergy' when they appear more serious, seem to be connected with both the protein and the lactose content of cows' milk. Even Cow & Gate admit in their promotional literature for infant foods that one in twenty Europeans cannot tolerate milk, and have predictably developed a soya 'milk' to fill this gap in their market.

But as well as the so-called 'allergies' to cows' milk, which appear as eczema, asthma and all sorts of catarrhal conditions, it is now becoming clear that there is a link between a high milk consumption and heart disease. Many subsequent reports have borne out the findings of the Royal College of Physicians' 1976 publication *The Prevention of Coronary Heart Disease*. Autopsies performed on child accident victims in recent years have shown large numbers of them to have already damaged blood vessels which would lead to serious heart conditions in later life. When asked for his view on heart disease prevention, Sir Douglas Black, President of the British Medical Association, is quoted in *The Times* of 12 June 1984 as saying: 'Milk is a major killer. It is nonsense to give it to children in schools.' There is now a large body of literature which condemns milk as a drink for adults. Certainly it seems that milk from another animal, whose chemistry and needs are quite different from our own, is far from being the healthy food its promoters have claimed.

Milk from a modern dairy cow also carries residues of the drugs and hormones used to make the cows more productive, not to mention the fact that concentrations of stored poisons increase dramatically up the food chain, so that milk contains much higher levels of environmental pollutants (strontium 90, fluorides) than are found in vegetables. Far from being a 'natural' food, milk has been consumed by humans only in comparatively recent times (6,000 to 8,000 years) and purely dairy herds were not developed in this country until the late 19th century. It is a great pity that our infant reliance on the perfect food has become distorted in adulthood to an addiction to such an unnatural and potentially harmful product.

There are many other ways of getting the nutrients that we need (and even other ways of whitening our favourite drugs, tea and coffee), and a varied vegan diet can provide them adequately. After a period of veganism, one does not worry whether one is getting adequate amounts of this or that nutrient, and I have found that, given freshness and variety, a non-animal diet is automatically fulfilling, even and especially during its severest test, pregnancy and lactation. But the new vegan will at first usually want to make a brief study of nutrition and cooking.

Firstly, the quality of our food depends upon the quality of the land on which it is grown, and therefore ecological considerations are inseparable from the subject of nutrition. Monoculture with the use of artificial chemicals has produced in our shops, for instance, watercress containing no iron, and oranges containing no vitamin C! People concerned for their health should be interested in where their food comes from.

(iii) The Protein Myth

Fresh, whole, organically grown foods are obviously preferable to denatured foods from factories, but aside from these considerations, new vegans, victims of a lifetime's habit of thinking of animal foods as our 'protein', may first of all panic that a vegan diet will not provide enough protein. People commonly think of animal foods as their source of protein, and are encouraged in this on all sides, from domestic science lessons in schools to popular magazine articles on cooking. Indeed, 'protein', to most British people, automatically means meat, fish, cheese, eggs, milk. There is no link in the ordinary person's mind between protein and cereals, pulses and vegetables – there is a complete blind spot here, as though vegetables actually did *not* contain protein. Over only a few generations, the meat and milk myth has blinded us to realities. And people subscribe to the popular myth, perhaps, without even knowing what this magical substance is.

In fact protein seems to consist of amino acids, that is, compounds of nitrogen and other elements, essential to all plants and animals. Therefore, grains and vegetables contain protein too! In fact, bread and cereals supply as much protein in the average English diet as does meat.[20] (And possibly in forms which the kidneys can cope with better than with the concentrated protein of animal food.) The question is one of the amounts and proportions of the nitrogenous compounds.

There are 20 or so amino acids all together, 12 of which are made in our bodies and 8 of which must be taken as food in order to sustain tissue building and repair. Grains and seeds are good sources of protein but have low proportions of two of the essential amino acids; legumes (peas and beans, i.e. pulses) have a high percentage of these two, whilst being low in two others. Therefore, eating foods from both groups at one time provides complete protein requirements from non-animal sources. Meat, soya and milk are foods which seem to contain the amino acids in good proportions, but the old notion of meat as first class protein is now generally discarded. Soya products and many nuts are actually better sources of protein.

In the fifties and sixties, scientists and marketeers elevated protein in the form of meat, fish and eggs almost to an elixir. Factory farming grew up on this myth, along with biology books that a whole generation studied – books which virtually ignored the possibility that vegetables, etc. might also be adequate sources of protein. Now the protein myth is in decline (though not, unfortunately, in schools, it seems) and we are told to replace the high proportion of calories obtained from sugar and fat in our diet with potatoes, grains and pulses which, as well as providing the calories, are also good sources of protein. 'With this shift in proportion [towards a low fat, high staple diet] you can maintain the present protein intake of about 12 per cent without being a carnivore.'[21]

As a vegan, you will not have to rack your brains or worry about providing elements of the two plant groups (seeds and legumes) in your meals but will automatically find they are there (beans on toast, stew and dumplings, curried rice and chappatis, peanut butter sandwich – peanuts are a legume). It is extremely unlikely that a normally well person living on a varied vegan diet in this country, satisfying his or her appetitie, would suffer from protein defficiency. With growing infants and children, slightly more care must be taken when they are too small to cope with the extra bulk often required in a vegan diet. Here, proprietary soya milks are useful, as are nut milks and creams which can be made at home (ground nuts blended into water). Tofu is also good for little ones, with its high protein and calcium content. Obviously, breast feeding is best for babies, and incidentally human milk has *less* protein than cows' milk. The greater bulk and fibrous nature of a vegan diet mean that the diseases associated with the lack of fibre in an animal-based diet, from constipation to cancer of the bowel, can be avoided.

Furthermore, information is now clearly indicating that protein in highly concentrated forms, i.e. animal protein, has not only been much over-valued in the Western diet, but also is potentially harmful because of its associated fats. It is much better for us to take our protein in the form of unrefined cereals and vegetables. Just one example of how this knowledge is filtering through from obscurity, where the manufacturers wish to keep it, appears on a diet sheet issued through the Sports Council to Olympic athletes in January 1983. This stressed that complex unrefined carbohydrates should replace the higher protein food, in the belief that they would provide better quality, energy and endurance in the athletes. 'Fresh fruit and vegetables increase the potential of the cells and improve the way the oxygen is used.'[22] There are many vegan athletes whose example bears this out.

Of course, the BMA, Sports Council, etc. are not (as yet) actually recommending a vegan diet. But pronouncements such as those cited are a great body-blow to the meat and milk myth.

(iv) Other Nutrients

Another over-played worry about the vegan diet is the question of vitamin B12. Years ago, someone whom I respected told me that this was 'the animal vitamin', and without it we would die. Given this terrifying information, I concluded that vegans must be mad and I didn't explore the subject further at that time. The whole complex story of vitamin B12 is by no means fully understood yet, though it is true that it is essential to our bodies. It is involved in the working of our nervous system and blood formation, and the consequences of its deficiency in our bodies are dire, with pernicious anaemia high on the list. However, deficiency is related more to other nutritional factors than to our actual intake of the vitamin, and is in fact more common amongst meat-eaters with a low intake of the folic acid needed for its absorption than amongst vegans.

The vitamin itself is manufactured by micro-organisms and is found in vegetables only when they have been 'contaminated' by those organisms. It is found in plants where microbes in the soil manufacture it and the plant takes it up (e.g. comfrey growing in rich soil, and seaweed growing near sewage effluent). As always, the quality of the soil is vitally linked with the quality of the food. Earthworm casts are rich in B12 (as are all animal excreta) and it can be taken up by vegetables under certain conditions, Commercially, it is produced by bacteria growing on vegetable matter. It is possible that humans have the ability to synthesise the vitamin in our own intestines and that this ability has been diminished by our turning to an omnivorous diet and thereby changing the bacterial content of our gut. Certainly, the constant dosing of ourselves with chlorine through our drinking water will not help the functioning of the micro-organisms which inhabit our intestines, and civilised 'hygiene' prevents the accidental intake of some bacteria from the environment. The early vegans who had never heard of B12 may have developed, or redeveloped, the ability to use the B12 produced by micro-organisms in the intestines. With so many variables and unknown factors, individuals vary greatly in their need to have a dietary source, so an intake of about 3 micrograms daily is a good insurance policy. This can be got from various yeast extracts (check the label – Marmite is not a very good source though it does now have some) or in tablet form. Personally, I have only bothered with a B12 tablet supplement whilst breast-feeding. Before 1912, nothing definite was known about vitamins at all and in our own times the research is still going on.

Another nutrient of particular interest to vegans is vitamin D. This we manufacture ourselves from sunlight on the skin, but if we lived in darkness our food source might be eggs, dairy produce and fish oil. Luckily the vitamin can be manufactured artificially by irradiating vegetable oil and is a compulsory component of all margarine, so vegans need not worry about this – again, there is a non-animal source of the nutrient, essential for its involvement in the absorption of calcium and phosphorous to form teeth and bones. At the time of writing there are several reliably vegan margarines, and these are readily available in health food shops. Sunlight remains the main source of vitamin D for vegans and non-vegans alike.

Regarding other nutrition needs, you can see even from orthodox food and cookery books that they are easily supplied by the plant kingdom. Do not skimp on iron-rich foods and remember especially the value of green leaves, the darker the better. Photosynthesis is the most important process on Earth and chlorophyll always appears in conjunction with various vital minerals. The beautiful colours of a nicely presented vegan meal will always include green.

The question of oils and fats is quite complicated, but since vegans avoid animal fats entirely we generally do not have to worry about it from the point of view of our own health. However, so-called 'saturated' fats (i.e. saturated with hydrogen) do occur in some vegetable products, as when oils are hydrogenated to change them into a solid condition, and with those natural products which do contain a high proportion of saturated fats, i.e. cocoa butter, coconut oil and olive oil. If you are keen to use polyunsaturated fat, then use sunflower, safflower or maize oil.

A nutrients chart is included at the end of this book for information, though, I repeat, as long as you have a diet with plenty of variety and include a generous proportion of fresh and raw foods, you need hardly bother with it. Needless to say, if you are pregnant or breast-feeding you have probably already made a much closer study of the subject. See Vegan Society literature.

(v) Why (Strictly) Vegan

Most vegans are healthy people who have taken the trouble to educate themselves about nutrition, and follow the way of life without necessarily giving much thought to it. But so strong is the meat and milk myth in our society than new vegans often spend an initial period in a frenzy to guarantee themselves the 'correct' amounts of nutrients. This springs from the reactionary thinking that the vegan diet is one that is 'lacking', rather than one that is in fact wholesome, nutritious and varied. As a vegan, you won't be 'making do' without animal products, but rather you will no longer regard them as food at all, and never think of them in connection with eating.

This might seem awfully 'strict' to someone who has not yet adopted a vegan diet, but, speaking personally, once I had made the decision to do without animal food I felt a sense of exhilaration and release from a cycle of exploitation. It was a very life-enhancing decision, and looking back on it now it seems that it was more like a liberation than an act of self-discipline. The reason why vegans are careful where possible to see that they never take animal products is not a sanctimonious attitude of wishing to keep their moral integrity untainted (though when I was omnivorous my suspicion of that in vegetarians used to put me off them), but it is usually because we think it important to illustrate to others that good health can be maintained entirely without animal products. To indulge even occasionally in milk or eggs, etc. would help support an industry that we hope to close down. (It is also true that after a period of true vegetarianism, meat and milk begin to seem horrifying and pathetic substances – certainly not things one would wish to consume unless severely pressed.) Vegans are still pioneers in the sense that we have to show everyone else that our common sense viewpoint and diet also foster happiness and good health.

On the other hand, flag-waving is a little off-putting, too. But it is necessary at times since the nation's eating habits will have to change if we are to survive, either in economic terms or as a nation of healthy people. Vegans are still unfortunately a tiny minority and the forces involved in maintaining the present food marketing set-up are vast, as we have seen. From the nutritional angle alone, the vegan case is clear. The biggest threats to world health are malnutrition in the Third World, and degenerative disease in the West. Both of these extremes are aggravated by animal farming, which must be wound down before true progress can be made.

6. Animal Exploitation

'I am a vegetarian for the same reason
that I am not a cannibal.'

Brigid Brophy

Supported by the facts of economics and nutrition, veganism is a matter of basic common sense. Despite its unfortunate eccentric or hyper-moralistic overtones, it is not a religion, though all of the world's great religions and philosophies have had an element of vegetarianism. It is also the case that a sympathetic awareness of human and animal suffering is a basic motive for many vegans. The raising of consciousness which comes about on discovering the horrific scale of human and animal suffering and waste gives veganism at least a humanitarian if not a spiritual dimension.

(i) The Realities of Slaughter

By eating meat, eggs and dairy products, we base our lives on killing. Slaughterhouses are terrifying places, where animals can die of fright before they reach the slaughter pens. 'A "shot" lamb is one that has panicked at the slaughterhouse in the moments before it dies ... its systems have burst with fright and it is virtually inedible.'[23] Farmers well know, too, that pigs can die of fright and so will feed them vitamin E to try to avoid heart attack prior to slaughter (cruel irony). On the other hand, 'Killing at a moment of fear creates a chemical process which lessens the growth of bacteria during curing'.[24] Evidently a fine balance of terror is necessary.

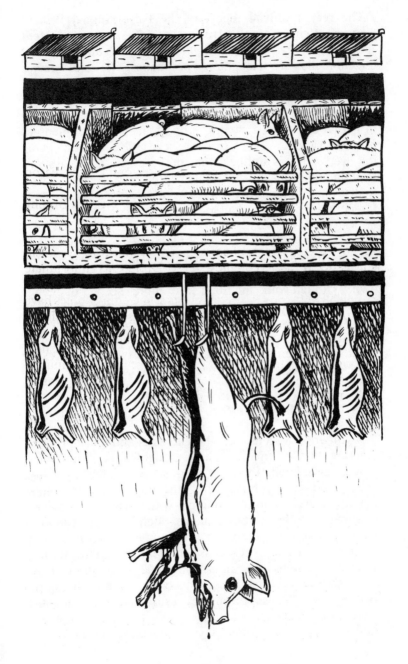

The recent official report of the Farm Animal Welfare Council, *Report on the Welfare of Livestock (Red Meat Animals) at the Time of Slaughter*[25] destroys any myth that the animals are slaughtered humanely (!) and makes horrifying reading. Even though the inspecting Council members always announced their visits, unnecessary cruelty was found at at every stage of the proceedings, from unloading to actual slaughter, for which the animals were sometimes fully conscious. Even existing legislation is not being followed, so it is unlikely that many of the Council's *117* recommendations will be implemented because of the meat trade's unwillingness to increase prices. We should never forget that daily mass slaughter is the basis of any diet that is not vegan.

In spite of what people would like to believe about 'dumb' animals, they have a perfectly developed nervous system and, faced with the prospect of slaughter, reactions similar to our own. Though our abattoirs are more secret than our cemeteries, our prisons and our asylums, and though we may try to forget, by concealing them, the millions of suffering creatures that we sacrifice each year to the meat and milk myth, somewhere in our subconscious or our nightmares we must know that it is 'Belsen every day' for the animals.

(ii) Conditions on Farms

If you are a 'vegetarian' who eats eggs and dairy produce, you are just as involved with slaughter as if you were omnivorous. Firstly, the sheer callousness with which animals are treated during 'husbandry' (the meaning of the world derives entirely from economics) which assumes that they exist merely to be used by humans, often has very little to do with care and welfare. To lose a certain percentage of animals from exposure may be less costly to a farmer than maintaining shelter for them. An amazing 16,000 large animals die unnecessarily each day (yes, sixteen thousand each day) on British farms.[26] This is through exposure, starvation, drug side effects or sheer neglect, and this fact alone is sufficient indictment of most farmers; if young ones are said to die from 'maternal' neglect, rather than the farmer's neglect, then that is because the farmers' inbreeding has neglected maternal qualities in favour of qualities of flesh or wool, etc. Farming methods account for many more animal deaths by accident than vivisection does by design. Veterinary supervision is not required by law in treatment of farm animals despite the massive reliance by farmers on medication, so that most vets these days make their livings from the more profitable household pets industry. A farm is the last place on Earth where a true animal-lover would feel at home.

(iii) The Dairy Cow

There are, possibly, a few people who still imagine that drinking cows' milk has nothing to do with the animals' suffering and slaughter. Actually the dairy industry has got the most blood on its hands. A cow has to be made pregnant each year to keep in lactation and a cow's pregnancy, like our own, lasts for nine months. As soon as lactation diminishes, despite a massive input of concentrated feedstuffs and synthetic hormones, she will be slaughtered. 'The ideal approach is to breed from the cow as early as is practical and take two to three calves ... It should then be slaughtered before it reaches mature size'.[27]

The calf which she produces each year will be allowed to suckle for a few days only, if at all (towards the end of a dairy cow's life her udder is so prolapsed that the calf cannot suckle in its natural position anyway). It will then be taken away (she will bray for it for days) and she will be attached to mechanical pumps twice a day to encourage and maintain her milk supply – obviously a calf would suckle more frequently than this. Any female will understand that the tenderest physical and emotional spots are touched, or rather brutalised, here. To encourage lactation when the offspring is dead seems to me most repugnant, adding insult to injury. And the net result of all this is merely the dumping of wasted whey over the fields which imprison the poor beasts. People generally think that milk comes in bottles, and they think no further. In reality, each pint of milk represents a degree of discomfort and distress – stockpiling or wasting the product represents mountains of suffering.

The calves (lucrative by-product of the dairy industry) have a pitilessly uncomfortable journey from the dairy farm to their horrific destination. The insides of their stomachs are needed for the rennet in cheese-making, and so-called 'vegetarian' cheese which uses a different enzyme ignores the fact that the calves have to die anyway, whether as veal or beef. Vegetarians who drink milk are blinding themselves to the fact that the modern dairy cow, who goes to slaughter prematurely exhausted, is one of the most intensively exploited and insensitively treated animals of our times. Our cattle are not truly indigenous and are certainly not a natural part of our landscape, the familiar breeds we now know having been developed in the 19th century and later. For pity's sake, extinction would be better for them.

(iv) Egg Production

But there is no end to human ingenuity in devising maximum profit from manipulating other species. (There is no species of farm animal that has not undergone generations of genetic manipulation. The poor things are all freaks.) For eaters of eggs, modern technology has brought us the battery hen, condemned to a 'life' sentence in her tortuously overcrowded cage until she dies of exhaustion or cannibalism, her uterus grossly prolapsed through the relentless laying induced on her, and never to glimpse anything except the suffering and death of her own kind. Even 'free range' hens hardly live a natural existence, and here again people have some pretty naïve ideas about farmers' wives merely 'collecting' the surplus eggs which nature supplies in abundance. The wild form of domestic hen lays only about half a dozen eggs in a series, possibly only once a year. She will not usually do this unless she has a mate – unfertilised eggs rarely occur in the wild. Having mated, the fowl will lay an egg daily until she has a comfortable number to sit on. She will then incubate and care for the young. She can lay extra eggs to replace lost ones, but this is regulated by the amount of food required by her. The colossal number of eggs produced by domestic hens comes about by the eggs being continually removed, and by prodigious feeding, nowadays with protein concentrates and the inevitable synthetic hormones.

What 'vegetarian' egg-eaters also tend to forget is that, like cows, hens produce male offspring in equal numbers to the females. For nearly every laying hen in existence, a male chick has been slaughtered. The details of this, in modern hatcheries, are not very pleasant. No rules govern their slaughter, since they are not destined for human consumption. After sexing, the unlucky males are sometimes thrown live into a mincer, to convert them into feedstuff, sometimes simply thrown into polythene bags to suffocate en masse.[28] The chicks destined for the broilerhouse are hardly less unfortunate. People who salve their conscience by eating only free-range eggs forget that this side of the business is an integral part of egg production.

(v) The Myth of the Hunter

Possibly plants, too, have an inscrutable 'nervous system' of a kind and in some way 'feel' and 'suffer'.[29] They are after all part of the sensitive fabric of the living Earth. But if you eat animals instead you are of course responsible for the destruction of many more plants than if you ate plants alone.

More than a thousand million animals are slaughtered each year in Britain. If I have not dealt closely enough with their horrific plight nor with the terrible lengths and depths of their suffering nor with the inconceivably vast scale of the relentless daily horror, it is not because I am unmindful of it, but because I am too much of a coward to dwell upon it for long, even in imagination.

Not many of us would witness the relentless daily and hourly scenes of sensitive young creatures being dragged and goaded, confused and terrified, away from their kin and into the slaughter pens, without our feeling great horror and equally great compassion. Not many could even watch the moment of slaughter which has to be left to a few case-hardened individuals. Even those rare people who kill their own meat, which seems the much more honest thing to do, usually have to steel themselves to learn the skills of slaughter.

47

Where, then, does our revulsion come from? The true carnivores kill without compassion (and their quarry is allowed its natural reactions of flight and struggle). Might we suspect from this that killing for food is not natural to us?

Though I would not wish to underemphasise the magic and ritual element of hunting that seems to have been a central part of some early civilisations which lived more closely with nature than does our own, the hunting 'instinct' has been much over-played in our culture. As we have seen, the meat myth has produced various misconceptions in nutrition. Two other myths are 'the survival of the fittest' (meaning 'the strongest', when it should in fact mean the most adaptable to circumstance, i.e. 'fit' = 'suitable') and 'man the primitive hunter'. Hunting is widely supposed to be be humankind's original food-finding activity, yet this is most probably not the case, as we have seen. The hunting theme is now tied in with the human self-image, which is unfortunate and also ironic, since certainly in Britain hunting has never been a vital means of survival throughout the centuries of recorded history. It has been the privilege of the rich and the last resort of the poor.[30] What does go back for many centuries is the domestication of animals, and not only for food.

(vi) Our Other Little (or Big) Captives

'How much is that doggy in the window?'

Animals have nervous systems, highly developed like our own, and intelligence suited to their particular ecological niche. They live and breathe as we do, and are in a sense our kin, and there is a residual awareness of this in the minds of those animal lovers who like to keep pets and are concerned with the welfare of animals, whether wild or domestic. Unfortunately the notion that animals exist for our use, or at least that we are justified in using or exploiting them, has rooted itself so deeply in our culture over the centuries that it has perverted this residual awareness into a sort of half-blind anthropomorphism which ignores the true nature of pets and the status they have in our society.

48

Domestic pets have very little chance of living a fulfilled life, in the sense of utilising all the faculties with which nature has equipped them. Every caged bird or rodent, every confined or restrained creature however exotic or mundane, is condemned to a lifetime of deprivation of its natural activities of food-finding, self-preservation and mating, and to solitary confinement from the intricate social structure of which individuals of all species are a part. To say that the 'wilder' qualities of our domestic animals and pets have been 'bred out' of them and therefore they do not suffer, is simply not true, and this is illustrated for instance by the speed with which a liberated battery hen will return to a more natural condition and start activities like scratching and perching which she has never been allowed and which generations of her family have not even seen. Every pet shop, every hutch, pen or cage, represents a degree of suffering to which our conditioning has made us insensitive. If set free, domestic pets would have no ecological niche and would quickly perish or cause chaos. Our love of animals has put them into a sorry predicament indeed. Even the dog, or perhaps especially the dog, in our society of so-called dog lovers, suffers endless periods of boredom and frustration for every hour or so that s/he is properly stimulated by work or play. And living in the close confinement of modern-day families, with all the stresses involved, has even produced the neurotic dog, who is either an unfortunate child substitute or simply a sufferer of an unhappy family atmosphere.

It seems obvious that all living creatures are 'designed' for certain lifestyles (only the lifestyle most suited to humankind is most variable and in question). That humans' extreme possessiveness over material things has spilled over into the weaker species, so that they can actually have the arrogance to say that an animal 'belongs' to them, seems to me a distortion of the natural order. To use the word 'design' calls up all sorts of theological questions, but to assume a natural order is surely tenable. Perhaps one day we will reject the notion of 'owning' animals, just as we have now rejected the practice of owning humans, i.e. slavery.

Meanwhile, the keeping of 'pets' is part of our culture, though to me it is unjustifiable. There must be something wrong with us when we live in overcrowded cities and yet confine animals with us for 'companionship'. And if we are true animal lovers, we would not wish to be responsible through the food we feed to cats and dogs for maintaining the slaughterhouses, which can cut their losses by selling the least attractive meat to the pet food industry. To keep an omnivorous pet, and to feed it on the dead flesh of other equally sensitive and intelligent creatures, is surely a gross irony. I believe it is possible for some dogs to be vegan when reared on the diet from an early age, but the cat is unquestionably a true carnivore.

It is a mark of our insensitivity and our double standards when the pet food industry in a nation of animal lovers actually props up the meat industry, not to mention encouraging the mass slaughter of such creatures as whales and kangaroos, which we are only just dimly aware of, as if it took place on another planet.

The relationship between a person and another animal can be a beautiful thing, fraught though it is with human-centred misconceptions like animals being 'faithful' and being 'good'. But with the modern-day 'ownership' of cats and dogs, this must involve the need for slaughterhouses, an evil which should outweigh all other considerations. Not all pets, of course, are carnivores. I used to have a dream of establishing a colony of vegetarian animals, a paradigm of peaceful coexistence where guinea-pigs and tortoises would potter about amongst brightly-plumed birds and other decorative creatures, without fear. But apart from the massive importation of grains that this little prison camp would need, healthy breeding animals outside their natural environment would soon overpopulate their home. There would have to be either a trade to local pet shops, with all the horrifying possibilities that would involve, or a mass sterilisation or isolation programme of the inmates. In my view there is no justification for tampering with other animals and their environment in such ways. My old dream now seems very sentimental indeed.

Zoos are another ancient barbaric institution which fill me with horror. Guy the gorilla (RIP), prisoner and star attraction of one of our most respected zoological institutions, whose family group was slaughtered in order to bring him to his new home, used to symbolise the utter hopelessness of the situation of animals like him. Two modern excuses for maintaining zoos (which exist primarily to make money for people – even a job after all is a vested interest) are for their educational role and for protecting endangered species. But to observe animals in captivity (even in so-called 'safari parks') is only an education in the ways of human insensitivity. Removed from their natural environment with its thousands of ever-present intricate demands, they can do nothing but sink into inactivity or patterns of repetitive neurotic behaviour. Surely natural history books, and films of animals in the wild, are a far better education in the ways of animals. And as for the conservation aspect, it is certainly more cost-effective in terms of protecting endangered species (i.e. many species, not just a few captive specimens) to spend money on preserving wild areas than on breeding animals in zoos. There is already a list of creatures extinct in the wild that exist in zoos, and for which it is virtually impossible to recreate a natural habitat. Protecting our few remaining natural animal habitats must surely now be the most urgent priority.

I assume it is not necessary here to go deeply into the question of circuses, and I welcome the fact that several District Councils have now banned from their land circuses which use 'performing' animals. I expect the fight against cruel circuses will be won before long, but for the usual economic, not humanitarian, reasons.

(vii) The Double Standard

If I have dwelt over-long on the issue of other captive animals, it is because I regard keeping pets, etc. as part of our assumption that we may use animals as we wish. (Not every vegan, of course, would agree with me.) People who use animals as surrogate friends usually eat animals too. They claim affection for animals whilst turning a blind eye to the brutality we inflict upon them. This is a double standard which permeates our society. If a farmer kept a dog permanently tethered in a small pen he would be liable to prosecution under the Protection of Animals Act 1911, yet for doing this to his equally intelligent pigs he may receive grant aid. Similarly, poultry are of course excluded from the Protection of Birds Act 1954, which makes it an offence to keep any bird in a cage where it cannot spread its wings.

Training for acceptance of the double standard starts early, with our nursery songs and children's stories (which provide a fascinating study in anthropomorphism and mixed-up thinking). We encourage our children to be fond of animals and to keep them in boxes, jars and hutches, and we grow up with a spurious love of the countryside, not seeing it for what it usually is, a defoliated expanse around the animals' concentration camps. In fact, insensitivity to animal suffering is the order of the day amongst country dwellers, which is hardly surprising. I can think of nothing more obnoxious than rearing and protecting animals until maturity, only to lead them to slaughter. Treachery is too mild a word for this. A society which, as we have seen, bases its existence on killing, must have a degree of insensitivity to violence. Slaughterhouse towns are known to have a higher than normal incidence of crime.[31] Perhaps the atmosphere of death which hangs over them, and which the animals can sense, works in subtle ways on the human psyche. It is a mark of our insensitivity that such questions are matters merely of speculation or academic study.

(viii) Conscientious Consumerism

> 'It is also true that a man sees more of things themselves when he sees more of their origin; for their origin is a part of them, and indeed the most important part of them.'
> G.K. Chesterton, *St Francis of Assisi*

Compassion for suffering animals does not begin and end with animals but acknowledges the ultimate unity of all life. Now, in Britain today, a majority of people probably do not know in their hearts that paper is trees, leather is skin, and meat is flesh.[32] But when we question what blood has been shed for the food we eat, we also question who has died of hunger whilst grain has been fed to our cattle, who has laboured on plantations or in mills for our food and fabrics, and who has crawled underground to fetch the ore which makes our trinkets, ornaments and nuclear warheads. The list is endless. No single question is really separable from the whole. No one can be quite free from the cycle of exploitation which keeps the economic system turning over, but by refusing animal products wherever possible – and this is quite easy where food is concerned – we can take a huge step forward out of the morass. Educated people living in the affluent countries inevitably feel some degree of responsibility for the exploitation which supports their relatively luxurious lifestyle, and the guilt thereby created, conscious or sub-conscious, could be one of the causes of our society's malaise. Giving a minute fraction of our income occasionally to some worthy cause may or may not make much difference, but becoming vegan is a way for us to shed at least some of the blood guilt, and achieve a terrific uplifting of consciousness. If this sounds too far-fetched to be true, then at least we can free ourselves from the discomfort of maintaining the double standard, where we can on the one hand claim affection for certain fluffy or feathered creatures whilst on the other hand enjoying the results of animal agony. Life becomes clearer and more logical. And, more important perhaps, by adopting the most ecologically sound diet we can dramatically reduce the amount of devastation of Earth's resources for which we are personally responsible.

'Nobody made a greater mistake than he who did nothing because he could only do a little.'
Edmund Burke

There are many highly principled people these days who refuse any Third World consumer product, and if enough people did this it would doubtless be one way of ending the cash crop economy which keeps many poor countries poor. There are others who buy only through an organisation like Traidcraft which puts profits back into co-operatives and self-help organisations at grass roots level in the developing countries. Whichever path we choose as responsible consumers, by becoming vegan we immediately reduce drastically the amount of Third World products we consume by not taking them into our bodies via animal foods. We need to change our consumer habits and then gradually the market economies will change accordingly.

The main obstacle to these changes being widely adopted, however, is not people's illogicality but their indifference. Most people, unfortunately, seem not to be truly concerned about any tragedy which takes place outside their own home or workplace (nor even about the possibility of a nuclear holocaust). The millions who starve in silence and the dumb victims of animal farming are not particularly high in their consciousness. But I think that the change is at least possible. After all, every reform in our society from the abolition of serfdom and slavery to the opening of public libraries and contraceptive services has had to overcome the fierce resistance of the powerful and the broad indifference of the majority. Our next reform must strike at the roots of cruelty, violence and exploitation. A move towards proper vegetarianism is the next step for us to take.

> 'If you are not part of the solution, you are part of the problem.'

7. Meat and War

> 'As long as there are slaughterhouses,
> there will be battlefields.'
>
> Leo Tolstoy

As we have seen, the food we eat has a very high cost in Earth's resources and animal suffering. Fundamentally, it is not 'good' for us. Basing our lives on killing creatures who have no defence against us damages both our health and our sensitivity. Our just reward for our callousness towards the rest of creation is not only the prevalence of incurable disease in the affluent countries, but also constant warfare, which we manage to contain at present in the Third World.

(i) The First Wars

As we are more physiologically akin to the frugivorous apes than to any other animal, perhaps once in the past we lived peacefully amongst other jungle creatures. The mythologies of most cultures have remnants of an awareness of this, and our own is no exception. Though I hesitate to quote from the Bible, where you can find a text which seems to condone almost anything, and many of them contradictory, it is of interest to mention here the very first instructions which 'God' gave about our diet:

> 'I give you all plants that bear seed everywhere on Earth, and every tree bearing fruit which yields seed: they shall be yours for food.'
>
> (Genesis 1.29)

55

Moreover, the Bible indicates that we should have 'dominion' over other species, which points to our duties of conscious stewardship. (And what is the significance of Jesus' avoidance of the traditional slaughtered lamb for his last Passover supper, etc. etc?)

So humankind looks back upon a long-lost era of peace and vegetarianism. There are many legends of the 'garden' which provided our food. Our word 'paradise' comes from an ancient Persian word which denotes a walled garden.

It could be that changing environmental conditions made man into a killer, but this happened relatively suddenly and so we did not evolve the 'rituals' which the carnivores have to prevent them from killing their own kind. Thus the peculiarly human phenomenon of warfare began.

Perhaps killing for food made our ancestors more inclined to kill for other reasons. Certainly, ancient history shows a conflict between the peoples of the settled agricultural regions of Southern Europe and the Near East and the more warlike nomads, with their flocks and herds, attacking from the north. (The biblical story of Cain and Abel is a paradigm of this.) It was the need for large areas of land for grazing animals which caused the warlike disruption of early patterns of civilisation. (I believe that the word 'war' comes originally from an ancient Aryan word meaning 'desire for more cows'.)[33] And the extreme brutality and treachery of animal slaughter, as meat-eating increased with affluence and 'progress', could have had a mounting effect on human acceptance of war over the centuries.

It is a sad thought that this connection between meat-eating and warfare is even condoned in our society; along with the meat myth, we have been conned into accepting that a certain amount of violence is natural and even necessary. Soldiers and butchers can be popular and esteemed characters, figures of true manhood and beloved by politicians and advertising agencies; vegetarians and pacifists on the other hand are popularly thought of as weaklings and cowards, unable to face the 'facts' of life and a danger to the true grit of our nation.

(ii) Food and International Relations

Since the ancient times when men first fought for land, the wheel has come full circle. Having destroyed the indigenous cultures of other nations in our rapacious search for more and ever more raw materials, food and fuel to feed the monstrous notion of the expanding economy, rich Western countries are in a position to use food almost as a weapon. At the time of the OPEC assertiveness in the early seventies the US Secretary for Agriculture spoke of food as 'a powerful tool in our negotiating kit', and at the United Nations general assembly in September 1974, President Ford actually threatened the use of food as a weapon against the OPEC countries.

It seems that the pattern of world trade which has developed around the sophisticated lifestyle and diet encouraged in the West has created a situation where the poorer countries, robbed of their self-sufficiency, are easy victims. The 1974 World Food Conference maintained that each country should be self-sufficient in food in order to resist unfair bargaining in trade. We have already seen that the easiest way to self-sufficiency is basing the diet on food which comes directly from the land, that is, not through the bodies of animals. There might be less tension and bitterness in foreign exchange if we traded only for exoticness and variety, and not, as in the case of some nations, for very life itself. It would be nice to think that trade encouraged good international relations, but history has shown that this is not the case. A return to self-sufficiency in food for all nations would be a sound basis for world peace. This is the ultimate aim of veganism. The rich countries must release the stranglehold they have on the developing nations whereby these are robbed of raw materials and supplied with ever more sophisticated war machines, to prevent rebellion from their own poor who are disadvantaged by the system.

With this awareness of our vegetarian origins, and the need to return to regional self-sufficiency, it may seem that vegans are more than somewhat retrogressive, possibly having a half-baked wish to go back to the Garden of Eden. This is not so. There is no going back, for we have destroyed a large part of our environment; and in any case growth and change are inherent in all life. We need to move forward with appropriate technology in the massive programme of afforestation which is required in order to heal the wounds we have inflicted upon the Earth.

> 'Eat not unclean foods brought from far countries, but eat always that which your trees bear. For your God knows well what is needful for you, and where and when. And he gives to all his peoples of all kingdoms for food that which is best for each.'
>
> Jesus, *The Essene Gospel of Peace*

Some degree of self-sufficiency is an ideal which has necessarily been part and parcel of many alternative movements. A regional self-sufficiency, and certainly self-sufficiency of all nations in staple foods, would be the vegan contribution to global political stability. At the local level, at least one British family of four has shown that it can be self-sufficient in food and fuel on less than four acres of land (details from the Vegan Society). This is *less* than the amount of land that would be arrived at if all the fertile land in Britain were divided equally amongst the present population. Unfortunately it does not seem that our agricultural land is about to be redistributed. Land reform programmes are outside the scope of this book, but it can be said that we are certainly a long way from a situation of each family having its own plot and producing its own food and fuel. Personally I do not favour this in any case. Exchange of commodities with neighbours seems reasonable and not ecologically unsound. Not everyone would want to spend a high proportion of time on the land, though veganic culture could certainly involve far less drudgery than animal farming, particularly in winter. Self-sufficient families or extended families are not part of my own ideal, as they might not accommodate the interaction and change that are a necessary feature of reality. The Austrian economist and philosopher Leopold Kohr writes of a 'cantonised system of largely self-sufficient communities', and this was developed by Fritz Schumacher in *Small is Beautiful*. These ideas seem more realistic, given the social networks that we already have. For the moment, regional self-sufficiency in staple foods might be our first goal, and meanwhile through market forces we can encourage the growers to produce what is good for us.

In a vegan future, with the science and skills already acquired, we could inhabit garden cities and villages which would provide food, recreation and creative employment for us all. Afforestation ideals go back as far as Plato, who spoke of happier times when Attica's mountains were tree-clad. This is now no pipedream. but something that we can and must implement, given the desperate urgency of the situation. There is no more land left for us to transform with animal farming into dust bowls or barren hillsides. It is time to halt the stockpiling of our beef, our butter and our weapons of mass destruction. All these will be obsolete if we can manage to let the Earth and ourselves survive.

(iii) The Future

I do not wish to underestimate the enormous changes needed to bring about peace on Earth. These are as basic as the food we eat, and run from top to bottom of our social structures. Different social structures would arise as the rich and powerful elite of the world's meat-eaters changed their diet, and new economic patterns would emerge. A whole new way of looking at the problems is needed.

'The money required to provide adequate food, water, education, health and housing for everyone in the world has been estimated at 7 billion dollars a year ... about as much as the world spends on arms every two weeks.'[34] This often-quoted statement summarises for us the gross misplacement of our resources, but by putting the problem in money terms it perhaps oversimplifies it, implying that if we stopped spending money on arms then the world's starving would be fed, and so on. Perhaps it is the spurious unstoppable logic of money economics which makes our governments subsidise farming industries which produce surpluses which are themselves expensive to maintain (assuming optimistically that they are not stockpiling for a nuclear winter in the 165 or so cities and towns which now have 'intervention stores'). We need a new economics of resources, not of money, and there are signs that this new thinking is developing, even at government level, in Canada and parts of Europe (e.g. Norway and the Netherlands). Even though our own governments and academia cling to the status quo, a conference of eminent specialists – 'The Other Economic Summit' – took place in London in June 1984 at the same time as the European Economic Summit (famous for its lack of achievement) and now it looks at if this alternative may become a regular event. This at least shows that progress is in the air. A country's true resources lie not in gold bullion, and the bouncing off satellites of urgent messages about the exchange rates, but in the richness of the land, and the skills and character of its people.

> 'A vegetarian diet is the acid test of humanitarianism.'
>
> Leo Tolstoy

For those of us who are now vegan, the pioneering work has already been done by those who lived as vegans before a wide network of wholefood shops was established and official research had confirmed the soundness of the diet, and by those who formed the backbone of the Vegan Society and produced the *Vegan Journal* with its brilliant articles and features. Indeed we are 'standing on the shoulders of giants' and it is relatively easy for us to achieve this more humane lifestyle which aims at an equitable distribution of the world's resources. People who think they are working for peace whilst still eating animal products, or who think they can forget the issue of animal rights and concentrate on human rights, have not got down to the roots of the problem. Countless people have already shown their awareness of these issues by rejecting meat as food. A recent Gallup Poll (spring 1984) sponsored by the Releat Company which markets vegeburgers estimated that there may be 70,000 vegans and 1,100,000 vegetarians in the UK already. Even the RSPCA, past masters of the double standard, who send their inspectors to the very cattle markets in search of 'examples of cruelty', voted at their annual meeting in June 1984 to recommend vegetarianism to fellow-members and to people in general.

All this is heartening, because it shows that human growth, as opposed to economic growth, is taking place. If we want to feed the world's hungry, solve our country's 'economic' problems and improve our health, then we must stop the heartless and unnecessary business of exploiting animals. It is the next step forward, though it will come, by eventual depletion of resources, whether we like it or not. How much better to come to it not via the dire poverty and distress of our country[35] but through heightened sensitivity and health, working for equitable use of the Earth's resources, an improvement in our environment and an eventual elimination of exploitation and warfare.

'Until he extends the circle of his compassion to all living things, man will not himself find peace.'
Albert Schweitzer

When the vegan diet is widely adopted and it becomes generally realised that we no longer need to use animals as food, a whole range of by-products of the slaughterhouse will cease to appear in our other consumer goods, including clothing, footwear, car tyres, photographic film and soap. It is well within the range of our ingenuity to produce fabrics and commodities from vegetable and some mineral resources which would be cheap and (unlike modern synthetics) ecologically sound.

As we wind down the whole business of animal exploitation, alternatives to vivisection already in use will be more thoroughly developed. And as vegans we would never dream of using, let alone killing, animals for our entertainment or our sport. The vegan landscape could release large portions of land to be wild or near-wild, where animals (including people) could roam free. We might even work towards a distant future time when animals would lose their fear of us.[36]

All these reforms, bringing with them massive improvements in our environment, would eventually and naturally follow on from the most basic premise of veganism, which is to refrain from using animals as food. On a wide and general level, as well as the individual one, there is a lot of truth in the thought that a society is, or becomes, what it eats.

61

8. How to Eat Vegan

(i) Changing Our Habits

The aims of veganism, then, are very high indeed, but we have to start somewhere and in this case it's at the kitchen table and as early as infancy.[37] The meat and milk myth takes root in our tender formative years. Most die-hard meat eaters are unwilling to give up the stuff that their mothers probably spent hours trying to force down their throats, it being an unnatural food for them and most infants having a natural awareness of this. But after the tricky weaning period (tricky only for omnivores) they have been successfully conditioned, and once conditioning to meat-based meals has taken place it is often difficult to eradicate. It seems almost sacrilegious to deny what one's mother gave one as the very stuff of life. However, once I had become aware of the case for veganism, though it took me more than thirty years to reach this awareness, I changed my diet immediately with no ill effects other than nostalgia. I know others who have done the same. (Though if you have a 'delicate digestion' there is probably something wrong with you already through a lifetime's body abuse, in which case a gradual change-over is probably better.)

Similarly and perhaps especially with milk, a lifetime's habit can be an enormous obstacle to change. Calling up memories of early childhood comforts, cocoa at bedtime and mother's milk itself, milky drinks provide a subconscious womblike cosiness to those addicted to white tea and coffee. However it is only in comparatively recent times that cows' milk has become big business, and we don't actually need a white fluid on our cereals and in our beverages. But if we can't kick the habit we can easily buy soya 'milks' off the shelf. They are expensive only because of the unfair excise duties on the soya ingredient – in terms of the Earth's resources each pint should cost only a few pence. We should complain to our MPs about this unfair penalisation of vegetarians, who after all are already paying through their taxes to keep the price of cows' milk artificially low (whilst low-income vegans of course cannot benefit from welfare milk tokens). Various 'milks' for use in cooking and on cereals can be made by blending porridge oats or ground cashew nuts into water, with a little oil, though they do not mix with acidic tea or coffee.

Tea and coffee, of course, are cash crops which prop up shaky Third World economies using near-slave labour, but as they are drugs, rather than food, they are not really the concern of this book (though soya milk does make a nice cup of tea!). Herb teas and home-made wines are much healthier drinks. As for the nutritional value of milk, I've already shown that we can get our protein, calcium, vitamins and minerals in abundance from the plant world, avoiding the risks of milk's fat content, chemical residues and synthetic hormones.

All the nutrients we need for health are provided in abundance by plants. The chart at the end of this book could be greatly extended if space permitted. Using combinations of vegetables, cereals, pulses, fruits and salads, endlessly tasty, colourful and varied meals can be made, which get right away from the dull meat-and-two-veg syndrome. In breaking away from the cycle of suffering and exploitation involved in meat production, we throw off old habits of thought in more areas than one, and especially in the kitchen. We need not be creatures of habit, at the mercy of vested interests.

People who cook need to get away from the idea of recipes as such. Unlike the serfs who threw off their chains only in order to share the indulgences of their rulers, we need to throw off the chains which tell us, through clever marketing agencies, what to wear, what to think, and what to eat. The meat and milk myth has led to the narrow vision of meat and its accompaniments, and a whole way of thinking of a meal as a set piece, following certain rules, which has to be prepared and served 'correctly' according to a recipe which usually somebody else has thought up. Having become vegan and thereby taken up responsibility for what we consume, we can now shake off the chains of the 'right' and the 'wrong' way of going about one of our most vital activities. Having learned what we need to consume in order to be healthy, and having found out how the various foods react when mixed, blended, heated, etc. (both endless and fascinating studies in themselves), we can now cook actively, not passively, and with energetic individuality. We can read recipes for ideas and to find out what other people eat, but follow them once only at most, to learn how ingredients behave with each other. The essence of our liberation from the blinkers of advertising and conformity which prop up the myth is to *know what we are doing*. Once we know what we are doing, there is usually no need to follow to the last gramme or even to measure any ingredient at all, once we know what certain amounts look like. It's much quicker to tip food straight from the jar or packet; it saves time and washing up and is thereby another aspect of our liberation.

(ii) Outline of a Vegan Diet

What then, do we eat you may say? There are many varieties of vegan diets, from those which include a large proportion of raw food, via wholefood diets through to those which use a lot of convenience foods and packaged foods. They are all unquestionably cheaper than a meat and dairy based diet, even if you buy over-priced soya milk and a few instant meals.

There is no question of a vegan diet having to be austere or boring; if there is any problem it is that the Western world has been blinded by the over-indulgences of haute cuisine (fat laced with more fat). The high fibre, low fat diet that we now know is good for us is in fact that of Southern Europe, India, China, North Africa and South-East Asia – so it includes some of the finest cuisines in the world. Though we cannot leap immediately to such exotic heights (and in any case we want to avoid using many imported foods), we can adapt our ideas on meals with 'foreign' ideas on combinations and flavourings, using food that is available in our shops and gardens.

Try to aim for variety and then you will almost certainly get all the nutrients you need. Don't worry too much about correct combinations of nutrients which work together, as they usually happen automatically, for instance – vitamin A and oil (margarine on a green vegetable) vitamin C and iron (orange juice and muesli, fruit and nuts) vitamin D and oil with calcium (bread and margarine), etc.

A great bonus to our eating is the use of sprouting seeds, which is well worth looking into. Punch holes in the top of a dark wide-lidded jar and fill it to about ⅕ of its depth with mung beans, soya beans or alfalfa seeds (not those meant for sowing as they may have been sprayed – any from a food shop will do). Soak the beans for a day, and afterwards rinse them as often as you can, using the perforated lid to drain off the water. Keep them in a fairly warm place if possible – the kitchen window-sill will do in summer. After a few days they will be delicious in stir-fried vegetables, or in salads, an incredibly good and cheap source of vitamin C, calcium, phosphorous and iron.

Nuts are a tremendous source of protein and you can make them into lots of different roasts and rissoles – though they are arguably better raw, as the amino acid lysine is harmed by cooking. But don't worry if you don't go overboard on nuts, or if you can't afford them very often (and here again, nuts are expensive only because of market forces, not because they are a rare and difficult food). Cereals, pulses and vegetables are also good sources of protein. There is an extremely wide and colourful selection of dried peas and beans to choose from, to brighten up your kitchen shelves and make endless varieties of casseroles, bean roasts and rissoles. Wash them first, and change the water during cooking wherever practicable, to reduce the effect of flatulence they are said to cause. This is natural, as a healthy human gut, which is designed for a process of fermentation, consists of a proportion of solids and a proportion of gases.[38]

Soya flour is very nutritious and a little can be thrown in with almost anything you are making. A vegan 'cheese' can be made by stirring into margarine or vegetable oil as much soya flour as it will take, and flavouring it with Barmine or herbs, etc. Tofu is another cheese-like derivative of soya which you can buy off the shelf or make yourself (see Vegan Society literature). It is very rich in protein and minerals and has many culinary uses. For replacing eggs in a cake, you could use a teaspoon of arrowroot for binding, a dessertspoon of soya flour for food value and baking powder as a raising agent (for a light cake use oil instead of fat). For the gelling and binding properties of eggs you can use agar agar, a seaweed extract which is extremely high in iron and calcium – a teaspoon simmered in half a pint of water will set firmly on cooking (arrowroot is the cheaper alternative which I use).

If you have time, you will want to make you own wholemeal bread, and this is always rewarding. If you are worried that you are missing out on calcium after giving up milk and cheese (though the DHSS recommendations are based on a dairy diet and are probably too high), you could add one teaspoon of calcium BP to each pound of flour when you bake.

A little on the negative side. Sugar is possibly one of the

most harmful substances we knowingly consume, for reasons which are now widely known, and so should be largely avoided (in our house we eat such huge meals that we don't usually have room for a pudding). Salt, too, is a product which enlightened cooks now use very sparingly, as natural foods already have a perfect balance of mineral salts, and an intake of sodium chloride upsets the mineral balance of our bodies – over-consumption of salt raises the blood pressure and is now linked with heart disease.

I am aware that I have not adequately answered the question of what vegans do eat. When people confront me with this, imagining that the absence of meat, etc. leaves a large gap, I am aware that my answers may seem rather vague – something on the lines of – 'Oh, all sorts … nearly everything…' I therefore pinned a sheet of paper above my oven and wrote down each day for two weeks what we were having for the main meal. The result of this may provide a few ideas for meals. Listed after that are a few ideas taken directly from what we eat at our house – other vegans of course will eat quite differently. And near the end of the book there is a section of foolproof recipes, to start off with if necessary.

(iii) Main Meals Over a Typical Fortnight (Summer)

◇

BEAN GOULASH WITH NEW POTATOES AND TOMATO SALAD

For the goulash, fry onions and herbs in paprika (a generous dessertspoonful) and oil, then add tomato puree, stock, etc. to make a rich sauce in which you then simmer chopped kidney beans. Heavily flavour the tomato salad with garlic and add a generous amount of parsley. ('Stock' to a vegan is not cube-shaped but consists of water extracted from boiled vegetables, or simply a yeast extract stirred into hot water – Bisto powder, too, seems to be vegan!)

◇

MINCE WITH BUBBLE AND SQUEAK

For the mince, fry onions with left-over diced vegetables, add stock and soya mince (TVP, 'textured vegetable protein') or chopped nuts, and simmer. Meanwhile fry the bubble and squeak (usually mashed potato and cabbage with marge, salt and pepper and a dash of soya milk) until nice and crisp.

◇

GOLDEN FRITTERS WITH SWEET AND SOUR MARROW

My golden fritters are frozen sweet corn, tipped into a small amount of spiced batter and dropped by the spoonful into hot oil. The 'sweet and sour' of the sauce (based as usual on fried onions and stock, thickened with flour and tomato puree) is achieved with molasses and cider vinegar – simmer the chopped marrow in the sauce.

◇

'SAUSAGES', CHIPS AND BEANS

Various vegan 'sausage' mixes are obtainable in health food shops. They also make delicious sausage rolls, pies, etc. Because they are relatively expensive I usually increase the bulk with boiled onions (using the boiling water to make the mix, and perhaps some left-over cooked rice, breadcrumbs, etc.)

◇

NUT CUTLETS, RICE, VEGETABLES IN SAUCE, SALAD

There are many types of nut rissoles, etc., but basically the mix consists of ground nuts, herbs, porridge oats (or breadcrumbs or wholemeal flour) for increasing the bulk, soya flour for richness, chopped onions, often fried first, for a savoury flavour and Barmine for B12 (add a huge teaspoon for flavour at the end of cooking to any savoury sauce). The rissole mixture holds together by the porridge oats absorbing the water and binding the other ingredients. Mould and squeeze it firmly with your hands (it can also be baked).

◇

BEAN ROAST, CHILLI SAUCE, SALAD, POTATOES

I usually do roast potatoes in the top of the oven when making any kind of roast. A quick roast can be made with tinned butter beans mashed up with tomatoes, herbs (e.g. rosemary, basil), oil, chopped onions and a little wholemeal flour. Barmine of course. Three finely chopped dried chillies added to a sauce based on onions, garlic and tomatoes will be hot enough for most people. Serve all this with a salad which is mainly green. This is a popular meal which I often give to guests. (They can put margarine on their potatoes if the sauce is too hot for them.)

◇

PIZZA AND SALAD

I usually make a huge savoury scone with white self-raising flour (adding wheat germ and soya flour to salve my conscience), a little oil, salt and water, and fry it very gently in a cast iron pan. The topping usually consists of chopped vegetables in a sauce flavoured with oregano, and this is spread over the huge scone pizza while the second side is cooking (it should be at least 5cms thick to serve three or four). Olives are delicious with this.

◇

STEW AND DUMPLINGS

Always start a stew off by frying the onions and garlic. This prevents sticking on the bottom of the pan later. Dark green leaves are usually an ingredient of my stews, and of one or more of the dried pulses. Dumplings are very popular (there is also a sweet version of dumplings, cooked in fruit whilst it is stewing).

◇

PEASE PUDDING, POTATOES, SALAD – THEN A DESSERT

We like pease pudding hot or cold, and it's useful at lunchtime. I often serve it warmed up with roasted vegetables and a hot chilli sauce. This meal was deliberately light because I had made a REFRIGERATED CHOCOLATE CAKE for a treat to follow – crushed vegan biscuits stirred into a mixture of melted dark chocolate, margarine, cocoa and whipped vegan cream, cooled in the fridge and topped with more vegan cream and almonds.

◇

MOUSSAKA

One version of this dish consists of new potatoes and aubergines, casseroled in a rich herby sauce of tomatoes, onions and garlic. Towards the end of cooking a white sauce is poured over and it's served when this is golden and bubbling.

◇

RICE BALLS, SPICY SAUCE, SALAD

Cooked rice squeezed into balls (add a bit of flour if it won't hold together), coated with sesame seeds and fried, is very tasty.

◇

PASTY, ROAST POTATOES, SALAD AND SAUCE

I often make a pie, or if I have time individual pasties, from left-over vegetables mixed with TVP, onions, Barmine and enough water to moisten. Naturally you would cook potatoes or something in the oven at the same time. (I also make a variation of flapjack nearly every time the oven is on, as this gets eaten up rapidly – it usually contains sesame seeds and currants for their nutritional value.)

◇

RATATOUILLE

Many recipe books will have versions of this, and it should be vegan anyway.

◇

CURRY

You could easily fill a book with vegan curries alone. I often make a hot dahl, or lentil curry, which cooks during the time it takes to boil brown rice, so the whole thing can be ready in not much more than half an hour. The fresh salad part of a meal is always welcome with a hot curry, even if it's only chopped onions and/or tomatoes.

(iv) Some More Ideas for Meals*

SHEPHERD'S PIE

Something tasty, casseroled and topped with mashed potatoes.

CASSEROLED vegetables are somehow always more delicious than a stew done on top of the cooker.

CHILLI without carne, but with the beans and possibly TVP, is delicious when cooked slowly in the oven, served with fresh bread and a crisp salad.

BOLOGNAISE to pour over your pasta can be made with vegetables cooked in a rich tomato sauce. TVP mince can be added for a nostalgic appearance, but garlic and oregano will give it an authentic Bolognaise taste.

STUFFED VEGETABLES

Potatoes, peppers and marrows are the candidates that spring to mind first. Rice, nuts, breadcrumbs are useful for stuffing, or of course one of the 'sausage' mixes. For a treat, a tasty sauce can be poured over the vegetables and they can be casseroled in this rather than merely baked.

PANCAKES

Sweet or savoury, stuffed and rolled or piled up with filling spread between.

*See also recipes on pp. 86-92

◇

PÂTÉS

Lentil pâté, hummus, pease pudding can be used in various ways. e.g. eaten straight with vegetables or salad, as sandwich filling, in pasties or pâté en croute, etc.

◇

CHINESE VEGETABLES

A variety of vegetables chopped into slivers and cooked quickly in a little oil before serving. I don't often do this because I like to relax with a glass of wine before actually serving the meal.

◇

SALADS

Don't forget fruits and nuts as salad ingredients. Try to include the various parts of plants, such as roots, shoots, leaves and fruit. If green is not a pleasing part of the salad itself, then if possible serve it on a bed of leaves. (A 'side salad' may depress the person who is washing up – I believe in huge dinner plates which will accommodate a salad alongside almost anything.)

◇

WILD FOODS

Even without specialist knowledge, many people are in a position to take advantage of dandelion greens and nettles (each spring we have a soup made from the fresh young tops of the first crop of nettles). These are plentiful and very nutritious especially compared with anaemic shop-bought lettuce – never pick from roadsides of course. If you have time you can read up on wild food and do a bit of exploring in your own area. I am lucky enough to be able to make wine from wild ingredients from spring to autumn.

◇

HAY BOX COOKING

We may be doing more of this in a New Age when fuel means more to us than quarterly bills. The hay box is an insulated box in which you can place a cooking pan so that it keeps its heat for as long as possible. I made mine with a wooden lidded box and many layers of newspaper. The pan sits inside tightly packed newspaper and is covered by a bagful of shredded paper packed in tightly under the lid. It is an old boy scout method and the principle is employed in various ways in the bush. Lentil stew works very well in a hay box as the lentils are easily cooked. Chop the vegetables more finely than usual. Bring the stew to the boil then immediately place in the hay box for six hours, or all day. When needed simply reheat. Ratatouille is also good with this method.

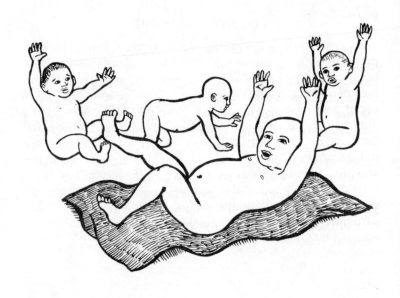

9. Vegan Babies

Another bonus of being vegan is that it reduces some of our qualms about having children. Since vegans use far less of the Earth's resources than do omnivores, population 'pressures' are seen in a different light.

(i) The Easy Approach

As vegans we believe that our diet which excludes animal products is most akin to what 'natural' food for humans might be. It certainly need not lack any essential nutrients and we are not doing without vital or useful foods. Therefore weaning vegan babies is perfectly easy and natural. Indeed I have noticed that many of the infant feeding problems which fill the pages of popular magazines are often associated with well-meaning mothers forcing meat and cow's milk down unwilling little throats.

In our society at this particular time, milk especially has wheedled its way into all kinds of foods and drinks and is particularly associated with infants and children. But for vegans, cows' milk as it appears in bottles for human consumption is an abhorrent substance, and we feel that it cannot possibly be a natural drink for us. I have no qualms whatever about letting my children go without it; indeed to make them drink it would seem to me an aberration.

It is true that in post-war Britain, the mass consumption of milk by young children relieved symptoms of severe malnutrition, like rickets, which were widely apparent amongst underprivileged children before that time. But it was wrong to assume that milk was the magic ingredient to combat malnourishment; it was simply the food that was used at the time, for reasons of convenience to politicians and farmers (often the same people). And now that milk is being discredited as a healthy drink even in orthodox medical circles, it is a pity that the government's only direct food aid to the poor is in the form of tokens for this unhealthy drink.

The thing about vegan infant feeding is not that it is specialist or difficult in any way, but only that it differs from the norm, at present, in our society. The difficulty lies not with the vegan diet but outside it, when most books on babies, and infant foods available, assume an omnivorous diet. Vegan foods are a minority amongst the masses of proprietary infant foods now available. And what health visitors usually recommend to clients is not appropriate either. Special baby foods in jars and cans, of course, are another marketing

(ii) Feeding Babies

There are several excellent and easily available books about breast feeding, which may interest you before and during lactation. The best guide to suckling a baby is just to relax and do it, and any minor problems you may have can be taken to your health visitor or NCT breast-feeding counsellor. The vegan diet is fine for milk production but do make sure you have an intake of vitamin B12, since lack of this vitamin could severely hamper the baby's development. As for other nutrients, they will almost certainly be adequately provided in the breast milk, and if your diet is inadequate this is more likely to be at the expense of your own vitality, rather than the quality of your milk. This is the one time that a regular B12 tablet supplement is recommended.

You will find you are drinking more than normal, so this could be a good time to experiment with different herb teas (raspberry leaf being the classic herb for this period of your life). My midwife recommended drinking Guinness, and I was quick to take up this suggestion (though apparently draught Guinness contains yeast with animal traces). You certainly do not need to drink milk to produce milk. The following is the complete list of foods to encourage milk production given by the writer on herbalism and natural living, Juliette de Bairacli Levy, in her book *Natural Rearing of Children*:

> 'Cereals, especially oats, barley, maize, all the onion family, all the pulses, all raw fruits, especially apples, pears, grapes, peaches, bananas, all the berries, especially black currants and rose hips, root vegetables, especially carrots, sweet potatoes and parsnips, all the green herbs, especially wild garlic leaves, spring onions, sage, milk, thistle, comfrey, chickory, etc. etc. ... all nuts, especially walnut, almond, pistachio and chestnut, all seeds, especially sunflower, sesame, fenugreek, linseed, celery, carrot, anise, onion and poppy.'[41]

con-trick, and are not necessary at all. We can easily do without them, and an outline of how to go about this is the purpose of this section of the book. Weaning vegan babies is perfectly easy and natural and should not present any problem. The real problems come later at butchers' shop windows and perhaps the school dinner table, when the growing child realises that s/he is living in a cruel world.

Every vegan who has gone through pregnancy and lactation will have educated herself as much as possible on vegan nutrition. (Health prior to conception, for both parents, is vital too of course.) A working knowledge of nutrition is the first requirement for weaning your baby,[39] as with omnivores. The second is a little ingenuity in gradually introducing the baby to your normal family foods with the minimum of extra food preparation time for yourself.

There are no hard rules on infant weaning since, like many other mammals, human beings are extremely adaptable. Baby feeding patterns and fashions have changed considerably in this country even over a generation or two. Nor can we look for guidance to child rearing in undeveloped regions, since there are many different patterns, depending on the diet and customs of the locality – the main overall difference being that breast feeding generally continues for a longer period in the developing countries.

Orthodox thinking in this country now seems to be that breast feeding is desirable (of course)[40] and that by the age of about six months supplementary feeding should be under way, to provide additional iron. Interestingly, it is also advised that ordinary cow's milk should not be introduced in the first year – another U-turn by the professionals! Since there are many varieties of vegan diet, from raw food to wholefood and even convenience foods, there is no one way of weaning vegan babies. It all depends on what your family eats, since the idea is to introduce the new member of the family to a diet similar to everyone else's. You should spend as much time as possible enjoying your baby, and as little as possible preparing food and reading books about it.

And this author is not a vegan but relies heavily on milk and eggs in the normal course. Rather than Guinness, she recommends a mixture of powdered sesame seeds and sweet red wine as a beverage during lactation. Much of the value of these drinks is probably in encouraging relaxation and rest, which is strongly recommended but not always easily achieved. Breast feeding is all that is needed for the first few months and the baby is the best judge of the amount needed and the frequency of feeds. It is impossible to over-feed a breast-fed baby.

Incidentally, two proprietary infant feeding formulas that have been developed from soya are not vegan – Wysoy because it has a small amount of beef stereate, and Formula S because it has an animal-derived D vitamin. Granose do a vegan infant milk in case for any reason it is required. Ordinary soya milks are fine when babies are weaning and ready to drink from a cup, though obviously it is not sufficient as a sole infant food.

It seems a momentous occasion when one first gives a baby something other than one's own milk. At this stage the additional feeding is not intended to provide the baby with basic nutrients but to get him or her used to the idea of feeding from a spoon, etc. to prepare for when it is needed later. Good foods to use initially are fruits (naturally) and perhaps root vegetables. Sieved ripe bananas, peaches, lightly stewed and sieved apples, prunes, pears and apricots are all suitable. Babies often like root vegetables, especially carrots, and it is likely that root vegetables have been treated with far fewer artificial chemicals than the fruits in the shops. A couple of spoonfuls of the cooked strained vegetable is all that is required at first.

If you want to see if the baby will enjoy drinking from a bottle, you could try offering strained fruit and vegetable juices, like apple and carrot, diluted with warm boiled water, or some fresh orange juice or the juice of soaked rasins. This is not actually necessary if you don't feel inclined to use a bottle, as breast milk provides all the necessary vitamins and fluid – it is a wonderful supply and demand mechanism that you don't have to worry about at all.

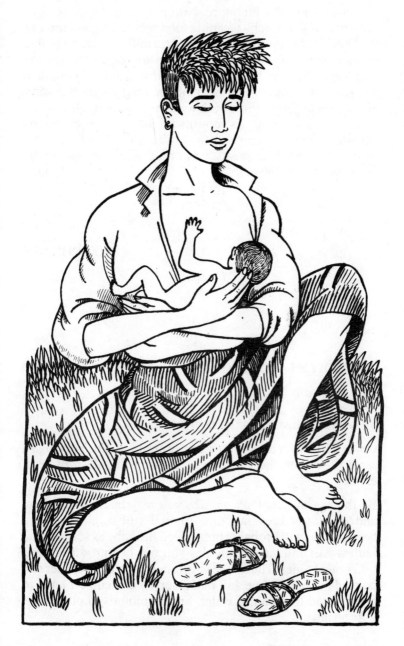

Baby cereals are often also recommended as first food – particularly in sales literature. Non-glutenous kinds such as baby rice or Farex baby weaning food would be good ones to try. They can be mixed with a little soya milk and warm boiled water, or some of your own milk if you are good at expressing it. In early times, cereals were pre-masticated by the mother, an excellent way of preparing them for a baby since digestion of starches begins in the mouth with the action of saliva.

By the age of about six months the baby will probably be anticipating and enjoying the solid food, and as s/he approaches the three meals a day routine might possibly be sleeping through the night.

BABY'S FAVOURITE DINNER AT 5-6 MONTHS

1 small potato
½ carrot
piece of cabbage leaf or sprig of parsley

Cover with water and simmer gently until soft. Push through a sieve (including the water) and stir in a tiny dash of yeast extract.

By the age of about six months you may be offering cereal and/or fruit at breakfast time (though not much is needed because you will probably breast feed the baby as soon as you both wake) and later in the day you will be introducing two other meal times. The above suggestion for a baby dinner can be made at lunch-time and half reserved in a cup for later, to be reheated in a pan of water. Small amounts of pulses can now be introduced.

◇

BABY'S MAIN MEALS AT 6-7 MONTHS

1 small potato
½ carrot
small piece of greens
1 dsp other vegetable – parsnips, peas or etc.
1 dsp red lentils (washed)

Cover with water and boil gently until soft. Then add a dash of Marmite, and blenderise or finely mince the food. This is done instead of sieving as in the early stages, because it retains the fibre, which the baby's system is now ready for, in this pulverised state.

Instead of the pulses, ground nuts could be mixed in, but babies often seem to prefer peas and lentils to nuts. Baby cereal can be mixed in with this vegetable puree, and also some tomato puree, which babies enjoy, and/or a dash of yeast extract.

By seven or eight months, when you are getting fed up with preparing special food for the baby, you will probably find that s/he is now ready to participate in:

◇

SOUP OF THE DAY

Fry a small onion in a generous amount of oil. Then add 2-3 cups of chopped vegetables (potatoes, carrots, peas, tomatoes, celery, etc. – enough for the amount you want), ½ cup of lentils or other washed pulses (which should have been pre-soaked) and a generous amount of fresh herbs or a pinch of dried herbs. Cover with plenty of water and simmer until soft.

When the vegetables are soft, take out two big scoopfuls for the baby, before adding salt and pepper for the rest of the family. Blenderise the baby's portion for a few seconds only, or mash with a fork. S/he will by now be learning to chew, with or without many teeth.

At this stage, pieces of bread can be added to the baby's food instead of baby cereals – the baby will probably prefer the taste and texture. For the times when the baby is sitting round the table with you, probably in the high chair, you can offer rusks. (Farley's rusks and, preferably, Milupa low-sugar fruit and cereal rusk, seem to be vegan. Bickipegs are also vegan and can be used from a very early age – though more for entertainment than nourishment.) By seven or eight months, bread and margarine with a touch of Marmite will be enjoyed, and you can stop buying rusks (dry toast is fine if you don't want to buy rusks in the first place).

During this period, the 'soup of the day' which you make with the baby in mind can be used in various ways for the main meal if you don't use it at lunchtime. It can be transformed into a curry, goulash or bolognaise, or mixed into soya or nutburgers, etc. – I have found it a very helpful way of minimising preparation time for the evening meal whilst at the same time providing two main courses for the baby.

Very soon after this stage, by about nine to ten months, the baby will be sharing some of your own meals. Just about all vegan food is palatable to babies – perhaps softened with a little hot water or soya milk – but concentrate on the vegetables only, if you are having a fried or heavily spiced dish.

Weaning is usually a gradual process and should be done not by the parent but by the baby. In my opinion babies should be allowed to breast feed for as long as they wish. After all, babies are the only humans who retain a completely natural intuition about what is good for them. If you allow the baby to wean him/herself then you will almost certainly find that you continue to breast feed well into the second year, often much longer. (But by this time of course the baby's solid food provides the bulk of nourishment and feeding is not so frequent as with small babies.)

There should not be any problems in child feeding associated specifically with veganism. (As I said before, the only possible difficulties come when the child confronts a world outside where habits are different.) Remember that in proportion to body weight, children's protein requirements are far greater than adults'. Soya drinks and foods are invaluable for this reason and most children will like them when nicely presented – possibly in naturally flavoured drinks, fruit mousses, and soyaburgers, all of which are classics for children.

Eating, after all, should be enjoyable, and children should grow up with memories of many happy mealtimes. If we could effect a large-scale change-over to a vegan diet, then perhaps we could all eat our fill without our happiness being clouded by the knowledge that in global terms we are a privileged minority.

Recipes

HIGH PROTEIN ROAST

1 large onion
60-80g. mushrooms
110g. red lentils
110g. ground nuts
80g. breadcrumbs
1 tbs. wheat germ

1 dsp. Barmine
1 tbs. soy sauce
1 tbs. lemon juice
2 tbs. oil
seasoning to taste
1 tsp. dried herbs

Wash the lentils and cook in water until soft. Meanwhile chop the onions and mushrooms and fry in oil. When soft, add all the rest of the ingredients and mix well. Shape into a mound on a greased baking tray and bake at 200°C for 30 mins.

A layer of sliced tomatoes can be sandwiched in the middle of this roast before baking, for variety. I usually surround a roast with partially cooked root vegetables and baste the whole in oil during cooking. Nut roasts of course can be eaten cold afterwards, though left-overs are unlikely.

STEAMED SAVOURY BEAN AND MUSHROOM PUDDING

Filling:

1 small cup dried butter
  beans
1 tbs. oil
2 tomatoes or some tomato
  puree
1 onion, chopped
½ tsp. mixed herbs
1 tbs. soy sauce
pepper to taste

Crust:

6 heaped tbs. SR flour
1 heaped tbs. wheat germ
1 heaped tbs. soya flour
pinch salt
3 tbs. vegetable oil
cold water

Soak the beans overnight and simmer until soft: 40-45 mins. (or open a tin of cooked butter beans).

Filling:

Fry the onion in oil with the herbs. Add mushrooms and tomato puree. When heated through, add beans, soya sauce and seasoning and simmer gently whilst preparing the crust.

Crust:

Combine all ingredients together in a bowl, mixing and kneading with fingers of one hand – add enough cold water to make a firm pastry consistency. Lightly grease a 20 cms pudding basin and press ⅔ of the pastry round the inside. Tip in the filling and form a sealed top with the rest of the pastry. Cut a small hole in the middle of the pastry lid. Place in a large saucepan in 5 cms boiling water and cover with an inverted dish or smaller saucepan lid, to prevent the top getting soaked. Cover the large saucepan with its own lid and steam for 35-40 mins. (don't let the water dry up).

Serve with potatoes, gravy and a green vegetable.

◇

VEGEBURGERS

1 tin red kidney beans or 1 mug cooked beans, well rinsed
1 onion, finely chopped
1 tbs. dried parsley or a generous handful fresh chopped
*   parsley*
1 tbs. wholemeal flour
1 dsp. lemon juice
1 dsp. soy sauce
2 tbs. tomato puree
salt and pepper

Mash the beans thoroughly, then mix in all the other ingredients, blending with a little water if necessary to achieve a stiff paste consistency. Form into shapes and fry gently until a rich brown colour.

Serve with chips, tomatoes and white bread rolls to visiting teenagers.

Follow with a fruit sorbet.

RISOTTO

Boil 1 cup brown rice in 2 cups water very gently for 35-40 mins. Meanwhile cook gently in another pan:

> *1 chopped onion*
> *2 tbs. oil*
> *1 sliced green or red pepper*
> *1 tsp. curry powder*

ADD   *cooked rice*
            1 can sweetcorn
            ½ cup salted peanuts

Stir all together. Serve with tomatoes, fresh salad and crusty bread.

HOT CHILLI SAUCE

1 tbs. oil	*½ tsp. dried mixed herbs or*
1 onion	*basil*
1 clove garlic	*1 tbs. wholemeal flour*
1 large (400g.) can tomatoes	*1 cup water*
2-3 dried chilli peppers	*soy sauce*

Chop onion and garlic finely and fry in oil, in a saucepan. Add herbs and chopped chillis. Dissolve flour in a cup of water, add to pan and stir. Add canned tomatoes, with juice, crushing them with spoon. Simmer until the meal is ready (at least 10 mins). Add soy sauce to taste (instead of salt).

LENTIL PÂTÉ

220g. lentils	*2 tbs. oil*
60g. breadcrumbs or	*large pinch dried sage*
* porridge oats*	*0.3l. water or stock*
1 finely chopped onion	*seasoning*

Fry onions with sage in oil in a saucepan. Add lentils and water or stock. When lentils are mushy and liquid absorbed, take off the heat, add breadcrumbs or oats (enough to make a nice pâté consistency) and seasoning. Mix well and leave to cool in a nice dish.

This is delicious in sandwiches and is also useful in pasties etc. You can even form it into rissoles, coat with flour and fry it.!

◇

PEASE PUDDING

1 cup dried split green peas
1 onion
1-2 tbs. oil
½ tsp. dried sage or dried mixed herbs
salt and pepper

Soak the peas overnight or for 1 hour in boiling water. Rinse, then place in a pan with enough water to cover. Simmer 35 mins. until soft. Meanwhile finely chop the onion and fry in oil with herbs until soft. Add the mushy peas and stir together thoroughly with seasoning.

◇

CHOCOLATE CAKE

80g. sugar
2 dsp. cocoa
160g. wholemeal flour
¾ tsp. bicarb.
3 tbs. vegetable oil
1 tsp. vanilla essence
1 dsp. cider vinegar
0.2l. cold water

Filling:

60g. marge
1 large tbs. syrup
1 large dsp. cocoa

Mix the dry ingredients together in a bowl. Put liquids and oil in a jug and pour into bowl. Mix together well and pour into two greased sandwich tins. Bake at 180°C for about 30 mins. – until firm enough to spring back when lightly pressed. Remove from tins when completely cool.

Mix the filling (cold) and use to spread on top as well as between layers. Sprinkle a ridge of nuts, biscuit crumbs, etc. round the top for decoration.

PANCAKES

6 heaped tbs. white SR flour
1 heaped tbs. wheat germ
1 heaped tbs. soya flour
pinch salt
water

Make the batter an hour or two before needed, if possible. Put all dry ingredients into a bowl with enough water to form a loose paste. Beat thoroughly, then stir in more water, enough to make a batter consistency.

Make the pancakes in your heaviest pan, using the minimum amount of oil – only enough to cover bottom of pan.

Pour in the batter when the oil is *hot*. Flip the pancake over with a fish slice if afraid to toss. In our family we eat pancakes in the kitchen and everyone who is old enough makes his/her own pancake. Serve with sugar, syrup, oranges, lemons. Other ideas for toppings will emerge with greater family involvement in pancake technology.

FRESH FRUIT SORBET

Whizz together in a blender chopped fresh fruits in season – with just enough juice to operate the blender. Reserve some whole pieces for decoration (but not apple or banana as they will discolour unless wetted with lemon juice etc.)

A nice dessert if the meal did not include a large salad.

FRUIT CAKE

Simmer in a saucepan for a few minutes:
 1 mug dried fruit
 ¼ mug sugar
 ½ mug water

Then add:
1 mug SR flour
1 tbs. oil
½ tsp. bicarb. of soda
1 tbs. soya flour
1 tbs. wheat germ

Mix thoroughly. Bake slowly for about ¾ hour, until a knife comes out clean.

The above is based on a war-time recipe when eggs were scarce. A much more wholesome rich fruit cake can be made by thoroughly mixing together:

220g. plain wholemeal flour
280 g. dried fruit
3 tbs. oil
160g. water

Bake slowly for about 1½ hours.

◇

BISCUITS

150g. wholemeal flour
½ tsp. bicarb. of soda
1 tsp. ground ginger
1 large tbs. syrup
60g. marge

Melt syrup and marge in a saucepan. Mix well and roll into balls. Place well apart on a greased baking tray and flatten down with the flat side of a fork. Cook until golden at 180°C (about 20 mins.). Allow to cool before removing from tray.

It is very easy to make delicious and light scones and buns, etc. without eggs or cows' milk. I always add a little soya flour for nourishment.

Flapjack is another standby which is easily made vegan (adapt any recipe). Nuts, seeds, etc, can be added for richness and variety.

QUICK CHUTNEY

275g. stoneless dates
275g. sultanas
275g. cooking apples, peeled and cored
275g. onions
275g. raw sugar

0.3l. vinegar
½ tsp. salt
3 tbs. black molasses
½ tsp. pepper
1 tsp. ground ginger

Finely chop or mince together all the solid ingredients, then stir in the liquids and spices.

Allow to stand, lightly covered, in a large bowl for 24 hours then bottle as usual (makes 3-4 large jars).

I always make chutney this way because it saves fuel and does not fill the kitchen with steam. It keeps just as well – at least a year.

Another delicious chutney is made on the above principle using the spent elderberries left after wine-making – they are still very rich in minerals.

Nutrients Chart

PROTEIN	Nuts (almonds and brazils especially), soya beans and products, cereals, whole grains, wheat germ, dried peas and beans, brewer's yeast, sunflower seeds, sesame seeds, avocados, peanuts, potatoes.
CARBOHYDRATES	Bread, cereals, pulses, nuts, potatoes (the body will use valuable protein for energy if enough calories are not available).
FATS	Vegetable oils, nuts, margarine. Some vegetables, e.g. avocado.
CALCIUM	Molasses, almonds, brazils, baked beans, tofu, wholemeal bread, sunflower seeds, dried fruits, watercress, beetroot, dark green leaves, parsley, sesame seeds, dried peas and beans, turnips, carob flour, turnip tops, some spices (the seeds).
IRON	Molasses, oatmeal, lentils, millet, tofu, dark green leaves, parsley, dried fruits, sunflower seeds, sesame seeds, soya flour, wholemeal bread, figs, apricots, brewer's yeast, bran, wheat germ, baked beans, soya beans, almonds, brazils, cashews, cocoa, apricots, hazel nuts, peas, whole cereals.
FOLIC ACID	Green vegetables, yeast and yeast extracts.
VITAMIN A	Carrots, dark greens, tomatoes, pears, lettuce, brussel sprouts, peas, margarine, peppers, spinach, watercress, cabbage, dried apricots, prunes, turnip tops, kale.
B VITAMINS	All the whole cereals, pulses, nuts, yeast extracts, oatmeal, potatoes, beer, wheat germ.
VITAMIN B12	Barmene, Tastex, many processed foods, e.g. Sosmix – check the labels (even Cornflakes have B12 added!).
VITAMIN C	Raw fruit and vegetables, esp. rosehips, blackcurrants, cabbage and all greens, oranges, all citrus fruits.
VITAMIN D	Sunlight. Margarine.
VITAMIN E	Whole cereals, pulses, vegetable oils, wheat germ, green vegetables, tofu.
VITAMIN K	Green leafy vegetables.

Notes

1. Oxfam, *The Facts of Life* information pack, 1984.
2. Oxfam, *Hungry for Change* newsletter, Nov. 1984.
3. F. Wokes, 'Plant Foods for Human Nutrition', 1.32, 1968.
4. W.J. Bray in *New Scientist*, April 1976.
5. Figures from Oxfam.
6. UN statistics.
7. *Vegan Journal*, vol. 31, no. 2.
8. November 1984, *ITN News*.
9. *Guardian*, 5 March 1984.
10. South-Western Water Authority Report, 15 September 1982.
11. In 1974, according to FAO figures, one-third of the total number of farms in England and Wales occupied nine-tenths of the agricultural land; 67 per cent of the holdings held cattle, 19.5 per cent held pigs, 27 per cent sheep and 35 per cent poultry.
12. Ministry of Agriculture, leaflet 400.
13. J.H. Kellog quoted in Jon Wynne-Tyson's *Food for a Future*.
14. 'During the 1970s African drought the Sahelian countries of West African exported 13,600 tonnes of vegetables mainly to Europe. Yet over 250,000 people died in the Sahel during this time because they hadn't enough to eat.' – Oxfam *Facts of Life* information pack.
15. Susan George speaking on BBC2 'Science Topics – Food and Population', February 1985.
16. *Guardian*, 28 December 1984.
17. J. Bronowski, *The Ascent of Man*, BBC Publications, 1973.
18. There is an interesting section on the health of various people who traditionally have a high intake of animal produce, like the Eskimos and the Masai, in Jon Wynne-Tyson's *Food for a Future*.
19. Kit Pedler, *The Quest for Gaia*.
20. Jon Wynnne-Tyson, op. cit.
21. Colin Tudge, *Guardian*, 7 May 1981.
22. Alan Lewis *The Natural Athlete*, Century Publishing, 1984 – quoted in the *Vegan Journal*, vol. 31, no. 3.

23. Drew Smith, *Guardian*, 17 June 1983.

24. Ronald Blythe, *Guardian*, 4 March 1982.

25. HMSO, June 1984.

26. *The Veterinary Record*, vol. III, no. 2, 1982.

27. *Farmers Weekly*, 10 February 1984.

28. This I know from personal experience.

29. cf. *The Secret Life of Plants* by Peter Tompkins and Christopher Bird – Penguin, 1975.

30. In fact, because of urban and population pressure, the hunting argument is hypothetical anyway. Certainly in most parts of Britain, it just does not fit any emergency situation in which we could imagine ourselves. I believe that to feed Britain's population by hunting wild animals for food, a land area more than that of the entire world would be needed!

31. Jon Wynne-Tyson, *Food for a Future*. John Bryant, *Fettered Kingdoms*.

32. Over 25 per cent of people questioned in a survey conducted by Animal Aid in September 1984 were not aware when eating meat that they were eating a dead animal.

33. H. Bailey Stevens quoted in the *Vegan Journal*, vol. 25, no. 4.

34. *New Internationalist*, Jan. 1980.

35. Early signs of the present disastrous famine in Africa were of course the killing and starvation of the animals.

36. 'Our future survival depends on our ability to recover community with animals'. Kit Pedler, *The Quest for Gaia*.

37. 'People have never had freedom of choice in nutrition. With the best of intentions their parents misled them in their youth and, with more questionable motives, advertisers misled them in adult life'. N.W. Pirie, *Food Resources Conventional and Novel*, Penguin, 1969.

38. 'Wind' is not a disease but a natural function of our bodies, and other nations recognise this. Also, veganic 'wind' is not unpleasant like the putrid emissions of the omnivores.

39. See Bibliography – *Vegan Nutrition* and *Vegan Mothers and Children*.

40. The Vegan Society has constantly been in the forefront of campaigns to promote breast feeding.

41. Faber, 1970.

Bibliography

General

Jon Wynne-Tyson, *Food for a Future* (Centaur, 1979).

Jon Wynne-Tyson (ed.), *The Extended Circle* (Centaur, 1985).

Kit Pedler, *The Quest for Gaia* (Granada, 1981).

Caroline Walker and Geoffrey Cannon, *The Food Scandal* (Century, 1984).

Leopold Kohr, *Overdeveloped Nations* (Davies, 1977).

Edmond Szekeley (ed.), *The Gospel of Peace of Jesus Christ* (C. W. Daniel, 1977).

Third World

Susan George, *How The Other Half Dies* (Penguin, 1976).

Nigel Twose, *Cultivating Hunger* (Oxfam, 1984).

Bombs For Breakfast, Committee on Poverty and the Arms Trade, 1981.

The Land

Anthony Wigens, *The Clandestine Farm* (Granada, 1981).

John Seymour, *Bring Me My Bow* (Turnstone, 1977).

Kenneth Melanby, *Can Britain Feed Itself?* (Merlin, 1975).

Nutrition

Vegan Nutrition (The Vegan Society).

Vegan Mothers and Children (The Vegan Society).

Cooking

Leah Leneman, *Vegan Cooking* (Thorsons, 1982).

Eva Batt, *What Else is Cooking* (Thorsons, 1985).

Animals

John Bryant, *Fettered Kingdoms* (Ferne House, Wansbrook, Chard, Somerset).

The Farm Animal Welfare Council, *Report on the Welfare of Lifestock (Red Meat Animals) at the Time of Slaughter* (HMSO, 1984).

Useful Addresses

Traidcraft (craft work and vegan food – SAE for catalogue)
Kingsway
Gateshead NE11 0NE

The Vegan Society
9 Mawddwy Terrace
Minllyn
Dinas Mawddwy
Machynlleth SY20 9LW

Compassion in World Farming
Lyndum House
Petersfield GU32 3JG

Henry Doubleday Research Association
Covent Lane
Bocking
Braintree, Essex CM7 6RW

War on Want
467 Caledonian Road
London N7 9BE